October Rain

October Rain

A Journey of Survival

Maynard Michael Clark

Published by Strike-A-Chord Books in cooperation with Lulu.com

ISBN: 978-0-6151-5924-9

Editor: Olivia Gorman

Format & Layout: Tracy Simmons

Covers: Kristin Simmons

Administrative Liaison: Suzenne Seradwyn

"To Be Alive" co-written by PJ Smith and Vivian Patrick Campbell © 1999 Purple Shoes Music/Vivian Campbell Music. (BMI) Reprinted with permission. All rights reserved. For more information regarding PJ Smith's and Vivian Campbell's music please visit their websites at: www.pjsmith.net; www.viviancampbell.com and www.myspace.com/clockrocks.

DISCLAIMER:
The events described in this book are real. All names and locations have been changed, including those in journal entries to protect the privacy of various individuals and institutions.

To order additional copies of this book, please visit: www.lulu.com

Printed in the United States of America.

$12.95 (USA)

To SMC
for musically showing
me the way home.

ACKNOWLEDGMENTS

To my "brothers" Sean (RIP) and David, thank you for sharing your wonderful light with me. Both of you were instrumental in helping me find my happy place. I miss both of you very much.

I wish to thank my current friends for their endless support, their hugs and for sharing a special yearly anniversary with me. I am very fortunate to have such special friends.

To Kook, thank you for always finding a way to make me laugh and for being Phil to my Steve. We may not be the "Terror Twins" but we sure know how to get into trouble. Here's to many more great years of laughter and conversations about Def Leppard's music.

I'd like to thank Olivia Gorman for editing my book and being a good sound board. Both of us have taken roads not traveled and found ourselves along the way. You've come a long way, Olivia.

Many thanks to Tracy Simmons and her daughter Kristin for their help in the format, layout and cover design of this book. There's a reason why I stick to writing, as I learned quickly that format, layout and cover design work is not one of my skills. Thanks for bailing me out.

I wish to thank Suzenne "Goddess" Seradwyn for helping me with a couple of phone calls and other issues related to putting this book together. Thank you for your support, even though I may have driven you crazy once or twice in the process.

Many thanks to Lyn Wakefield, MACP, for her support in this endeavor as I heal and understand how I managed to survive my ordeal. Thank you for never letting me forget how strong I really am.

Finally, I'd like to thank PJ Smith and Vivian Campbell for allowing me to share their lyrics from "To Be Alive" with all of you. *Go raibh maith agat*!

People dance in and out of our lives all the time. Some of them stay with us as life long reminders that we are all worthy to be alive, to be happy and enjoy life. These people share something wonderful with all of us. They share a part of themselves that often speaks to us on a much deeper level. To the members of Def Leppard, Megadeth, Metallica, and the many other bands and musicians who have inspired me through the years, thank you for sharing your intimate gift of music. Your music guided me through some very dark times. Thank you for making music that not only makes people happy but also reminds us to never give up on ourselves.

TABLE OF CONTENTS

"To Be Alive"

And I don't think that it's right
To let love pass by
Any time of life
It's good to be alive.

INTRODUCTION

Fifteen years ago I made an attempt to take my own life. It was the last attempt in a series of seven over a four year period. Though I think about those days often, the actual intent to kill myself has not surfaced for a long time. Those depressed, pill-popping, alcohol driven attempts of suicide are a thing of my past but they are not easily forgotten. For a segment of seven years I wasted my life in depression and suicide. I tried lighting myself on fire, on four different occasions I drank heavily and mixed in some Tylenol, I cut myself with a plastic knife and I also stood on a roof contemplating whether or not to jump. One question that has popped up has been, why? Why did I want to kill myself? It's a really good question and one that even after all these years I cannot easily answer. I'm going to attempt to answer that question, although I know that I'll have to revisit a dark place and feel emotions that will definitely hurt me. Life just sucked back then. I know the superficial reasons why, but the deep inner reasons have been buried for a long time.

I have worked hard to be the person I am today. However, I acknowledge my past and after all these years I am still learning from my suicidal experiences. I am a suicide survivor. It is my hope that fellow suicide survivors who have turned their lives around will claim this statement for themselves. I may be seen as weak, but I'll tell you it takes a great deal of strength to fight the thoughts of killing yourself to see another day. It is not an easy journey to go from wanting to kill yourself to not killing yourself. There is a constant internal struggle, and as much as you want to end your life there is a part of you that you may not be aware of trying to keep you alive. That's what happened to me. Somewhere deep inside me was an unspoken language of hope, belief and truth that came alive due to music.

I cry almost everyday only because there is still a lot of pain buried deep inside me, and maybe it's about time that I give that pain life and let it out. The journey I'm about to go on is one of an inner journey: an examination of self if you will. This is not a journey that can be taken lightly for the

1

scars that await me will be painful to cut open again. I know that I will not be alone on this journey for I have many wonderful people who inspire me and who care about me to support me in this endeavor. Some of these people are alive and some of them are…well, dead.

Whether alive or dead, people inspire me and give me strength in many ways. I will write about these important people and while some may seem silly, they are not. Each person is a representation of something bigger, something mystical in some cases. Don't worry folks; you'll see what I mean later on.

I'm sure my story will cause you, the reader, to feel a range of emotions. Know that these feelings are okay to have. Most of all, out of everything you feel I hope you come to a place of understanding. That's all I ask you: to simply understand. I can in no way make you feel exactly what I felt but I'll try and bring you as close as I can.

By bringing you into my world, I realize it is a risk to expose myself this way, but it's time to repair the damage done in my youth so I can enjoy the life I have now even more. In order to tell this story, my story, I have given voice to *Inner Me* who will appear in italics and a part of me I call the **Saboteur** who will appear in bold. At times their dialogue will be directed toward you, the reader, and at other times more focused on me, the person in the hot seat. In order to present this mess of a life I had, it is important that I give voice to these parts of myself in order to give you a more complete view of what I went through.

So where does this story begin? Good question, for even I'm unsure how this will all unfold. I do know that to start this journey I have to go to the end first and then revisit the beginning. So let me take you to my last suicide attempt; let me take you back to October 14th, 1992 and tell you about the person who changed my life.

CHAPTER ONE

"I Never Liked The Rain Until I Walked Through It With You" – Clint Black

October 14th, 1992 was the last time I made an attempt to take my own life. I was a senior at Caledonia State College. In the rain on that cold October night, I stood on top of the library roof looking down at the sidewalk and pond that were in my sight. I should explain that the library roof also served as a patio walkway to get to other parts of the campus and of course as I stood there looking over the edge no one thought twice when they passed me by.

On this particular night I contemplated killing myself, I looked over the edge in the rain wondering what I should do. Do I jump or do something else? Unlike my other attempts I was sober for this one, my mind a jumbled mess, my thoughts like unconnected puzzle pieces. With the rain coming down, a stranger had walked out of a nearby door and said "don't jump." How did they know what I was thinking? I was being pulled in all sorts of directions inside; to jump or not to jump was the question. In the darkness, under a lighted walkway lamp a friendly face in a black trench coat came walking. It was my friend Maggie. With tears in my eyes and the rain pelting me, Maggie led me to a person who could help me, someone who I had only known for a month, a relative stranger. When I met this person for the first time they seemed familiar, like an old friend had stepped back into my life. I was so full of misery but it wouldn't stay too long for the universe had heard my repeated un-vocalized cries for help. The universe sent me Michael Elliott.

Michael Elliott was born in December of 1971 and like me, he was a tortured soul. Both of us came from dark places but he showed his externally while I internalized mine. School officials tried to keep us apart because one of Michael's dark little secrets was that he had been institutionalized. Michael never told me how long he'd been institutionalized but I suppose a guy like him hanging out with a person like me might have seemed like a warning sign to a lot of people. The thing was we were the perfect match for each other. Michael was not only my friend but in some ways he was the brother I always wanted or more importantly the brother I needed.

On that rainy night we walked over two miles round-trip, the Cumberland Farms being mid-point where Michael bought some snacks. During our trek in the darkened rain, I opened up to Michael and let the pain that was in me come out. The vulnerable little girl encased in the body of a twenty-one year old college student was allowed to speak. Michael listened to me talk, he comforted me and above all he did not judge or ridicule me. He accepted me for who I was.

We had a unique friendship, one that I have not had with anyone else. Never have I had a friend that I could openly reveal my most inner thoughts and feelings to. Michael knew my weaknesses, the buttons to push and even with that knowledge of how to hurt me, he never used it against me. I believe he never did use what he knew because he knew I was equally armed with some secrets of his. He dated three of my friends but left me alone. Never did he attempt to have a relationship of that kind with me.

Ours was a relationship with meaning. It wasn't barren and superficial, if anything it was full of magic. With Michael I found my spiritual side and danced into the world of the paranormal but most of all I entered the dance of life.

A few weeks after my walk with Michael, there was a night where a bunch of friends and I, along with Michael gathered to play with a Ouija board. It was the "in" thing at the time. After that night, my friends seriously thought I was nuts. Throw in my friendship with Michael, and a case for me to be institutionalized grew a little stronger. My friends actually went to the school counselor to report that they thought I should be locked up and that Michael was warping my mind. I admit I thought I was going nuts at one point due to all the things that were happening but I was going through a transformation. I was trying to find myself, trying to reclaim a part of me that had been buried for years. I would not have been able to do it had it not been for Michael. He was my anchor. With Michael's help I truly felt alive for once. Everything seemed so brand new and much brighter compared to the darkened forest of suicidal thoughts I had been living in.

For the record, Michael was not as innocent as I make him out to be. He did a lot of good but unfortunately for all the good he did, he wiped it out with his insensitive heart. Michael was a cold person to a lot of people which was always a mystery to me. Wherever there was destruction, you knew Michael had just recently swept through. One of the more mysterious parts of his personality I guess. He never pulled any stunts with me but pulled plenty on everyone else. He had an agenda and under the category of "Lie & Cheat" was a long list of names of mutual friends he tricked, lied to, cheated on or cheated with and anything else you could possibly think of. However my name wasn't on the "Lie & Cheat" list. He didn't play such games with me.

At one point I did stop talking to him, going along with the group and being one of the gang. Michael basically got caught cheating on his girlfriend who happened to be a friend of mine. The girl that he was going to sleep with was also a friend but they had planned in advance to catch Michael being a low life scumbag.

There in front of me was the trap they laid for him and he took the bait. After that he got the cold shoulder from everyone, including me, and I hated doing that to him. The group would walk by him and he'd look and while the group continued on walking I'd always stop to look at him. I think he understood my need to be with the gang even though I hated myself for abandoning him after all he did for me. Everyone in the group ended their friendship with him but I never did. Unlike everyone else, I still cared for him and he knew that. He knew our friendship was one that would last forever.

Michael, Michael, Michael...what can be said about him that she hasn't already? Plenty I suppose. Losing touch with him after college bugged the hell out of her and quite honestly, me too. For a moment in time, several months really he was something that had been missing in our lives for a long time. Something neither of us wanted to see go. For all the pain he inflicted on others and even us, deep down it didn't matter what anyone said really, he embodied our inner hopes and wishes.

He was the knight without the shining armor and horse. He was the big brother, the protector, the friend, the companion, the trickster and the cheat. He gave a glimmer of hope to us to show that the world didn't have to be so damn dark. Then again we thrive in the dark.

Most people run away from the dark and toward the light. Not us, we just sit here as if we're enjoying an afternoon tea in the English countryside. Michael saw Death, he knew what it looked like and so did we. Neither of us were scared to see it. Instead of running away like most, we welcomed Death. Once you start talking to Death, you realize there really is nothing to be scared about and to be honest Death really doesn't want us to die, not before our time anyway.

Michael was an important fixture in our lives. As much as I live inside this sometimes tormented body, Michael was the first step in healing. He listened to us, he cared for us, he understood the call of darkness and he understood what it was like to be rejected by society, to be cast out of the norm. Michael had a passion for vampires and depending on your view, you could say he had a passion for life. He never drank blood but if vampires were real, and who's to say they aren't although I have yet to meet one, Michael would have happily joined them. There are darker forces out there and Michael was definitely dark as were we when he stepped into our lives. They say two wrongs don't make a right and so two darks shouldn't make a light but with

Michael – it happened. We both transformed ourselves for each of us had something to offer the other. Michael gave us all the things we needed: unconditional love, friendship, a sense of self worth and a sense of family.

When Michael went his way and we went ours there was a deep sense of loss. Even now, years gone by, we miss him very much. I cannot think of accurate words to describe this feeling of loss. There is a song lyric that goes "We were always the better part of me." This is the closest that I can describe what Michael meant to us. His impact on us was that great. He made us feel whole and to not have him around makes us feel incomplete.

When we learned of Michael's death a few years ago we cried hard. We wailed in pain for it was a hurt we had not experienced for a long time. Michael was the first step in our recovery and to learn of his passing made us realize the important impact he had on our life.

For all the bad, cruel, disgusting things he did to others, what he did in kindness to us, from the goodness that was in him, from the side that knew of unconditional love, he gave us life. People can tear him to pieces and insult him but it will never change the acknowledgement and appreciation we have for him. He was all the things missing from our childhood, the things mommy and daddy neglected to do for us.

As the little girl who resides in this thirty-six year old body, I am ever thankful to have met such a person like Michael and to call him friend. Out of all the friends we have had, he was and is the best. The importance of Michael Elliott will never be forgotten for we will always love him for all time.

You two are pitiful. Michael was nothing more than a manipulative punk from Connecticut who thought he was above everyone else. Nothing but a lying cheat, a conniving jackass who did things for his own pleasure. Screw the world was his motto. Can't believe you two pine for him, he was an ass.

Yes, it's true Michael is that important to me, I mean us. I think of him often and can sense him sometimes. I miss him dearly, and especially miss his hugs because when he hugged me, my whole body filled up with this incredible warmth.

Every time he hugged me I never wanted to let go because it felt that good. In Michael's arms I felt safe and like nothing could ever harm me. I miss that connection with him and miss being held that way. I miss the kind of friendship I had with him and wish I could have it again.

CHAPTER TWO

"Light My Fire" – The Doors

It was the fall of 1988, my senior year at South Addison High School. This year would mark my fourth year of being depressed and the arrival of something I did not see coming. Unknown to those around me - friends, parents, teachers, guidance counselors - a dark demon lived inside of me. I never showed how depressed I was for I wore a mask to hide the pain that was in me. High school is a cruel time in a person's life. When we're small children we don't have the resources or the mechanisms to defend ourselves when we're told "you're ugly" by someone else. We don't have the necessary skills to process that and by our teenage years, those early negative comments and situations get embedded into our brains and run like a tape machine to be played over and over again.

For some kids, the tape machine stops and for others, like me, it plays over and over and more just gets added to it. I was never good enough for anyone and I never really fit in. I was an only child so I was used to being by myself, and that may have been the problem, too.

Take an extremely shy kid whose parents didn't necessarily show the parental interest they should have, who constantly argued all the time making their kid wonder if divorce was around the corner. Throw in a hostile teenage school environment and you have a volatile situation brewing. Talk about an unstable environment to grow up in. Not to mention that the high school you are attending is filled with kids whose mommies and daddies have high pay- ing jobs and can afford to clothe their kids in the latest fashions. Not only did I get picked on for being "ugly" by my classmates, but my wardrobe was also a topic of scrutiny, as my mom didn't work and my dad had his own busi- ness. We lived below the poverty line but mom and dad always made sure that there was food, shelter and that I had clothes to wear. The day I showed up wearing something that was "in" fashion at school, one of the snobby girls actually told me it was about time I joined the rest of the world. I was an easy target for my classmates; seek and destroy seemed like a game that was played everyday by them. I admit I probably didn't help matters by being shy. Unfortunately, my shyness seemed to translate into me being a bitch which wasn't the case. I was just quiet. I was the kid who ate lunch by herself. I was the kid who barely had any friends. I was that kid who didn't fit in with the misfits and didn't fit in with the popular kids. I was on the fence. It's easy to see how all the abusive internal comments grew in strength.

You had to dig it up didn't you? High school was horrible. It was one giant rejection. Didn't meet the standards of the fashion police, didn't meet the standards of looking pretty, didn't meet the standards of mommy and daddy and certainly didn't meet the standards of being someone to call a friend. We walked through high school with a knife in us, a fragile little girl with no where to go for help. We were lost in the woods looking for a way home - looking for a place of sanctuary and never finding it.

If there was ever a time in our lives where we were less than authentic it was high school. We hid everything about ourselves in order to just get through it. No one ever suspected quiet little us as being depressed since we didn't cause any problems in class, we were always on time and our grades were average as usual. There was nothing to indicate that there was a serious problem brewing. We went about our business as the invisible girl. Things went down hill when feelings surfaced about Tony, your best friend's boyfriend. That was the clincher in us taking that first step down the dark path of worthlessness.

I have always had a hard time with the concept of self-worth. For the longest time I didn't think or believe I was worthy of anything. In high school I didn't think I was worthy to have a boyfriend, worthy to have any friends, worthy to be happy and most of all worthy to be alive. I thought I was a big waste of everyone's time and that if I killed myself then everything would be fine. Seriously, these thoughts just snowball and get reinforced. For example, I had asked three different guys to the prom and all three said no. The train was full speed ahead on the negativity track. Rejected three times gets turned internally that I'm ugly, not worthy, not anything. In high school you aren't armed to tell yourself that it's not you, it's them.

I admit now, looking back, that a game was going on. How much can I show yet still not be seen. My game was a way to see my worth. How much did I have to show of my pain before someone noticed? In high school, no one noticed. No teachers, no guidance counselors, no friends except maybe two. I was ignored at home and at school. It's hard to feel good about yourself when you're invisible.

Clues were there that I was in trouble yet no one paid attention. So the thoughts and feelings of "I'm not worthy," "I'm not important" and "No one will miss me", "No one loves me," were just compounded over and over.

I'm not sure when the first thoughts of killing myself surfaced exactly but they had obviously been growing inside me. I remember having dreams of killing myself by jumping off a building or driving a car off a cliff.

The thing is I would feel somewhat better the next morning. These "killing myself off" dreams were frequent for me. It was like I was trying to ditch all the bad things that had been stuck to me over the years. I was killing myself off trying to find the real me I suppose. In these dreams I would see myself get killed from a distance or actually feel like I was falling and would watch the pavement kiss my face.

The train derailment kicked into gear when my friend Elisa Kennedy began dating my friend Tony McKay. Tony was a riot. He was funny, liked the same music as me and was just a great guy to hang out with. Then something surfaced in me, something I didn't know how to handle because I had no prior experience to help me deal with it.

I started to have feelings about Tony. I liked him so much that I was wishing we were an item. The more time I spent hanging out with him and the rest of my friends the more I wanted to be with him. It was tearing me up inside because I felt that I was betraying Elisa by having these feelings.

The internal conflict was a nightmare and that's when the darkness reached out to me in a way it never had before. I was berating myself for the feelings I was having and on a cold May night I made my first suicide attempt. I had been hanging out with Tony and Elisa when we headed back to her townhouse to hang outside for awhile.

I remember Tony pushing Elisa on the swing set before quietly disappearing behind one of the townhouses to end my life. It's been a long time since that night and the sequence of events is almost gone from my memory except for the way I tried to take my life. What I do remember was trying to light the shirt I was wearing on fire. Where or how I got the idea to end my life by fire I honestly don't know and while I managed to get a thread on my shirt lit, it quickly fizzled out. The only thing I managed to burn besides one measly little thread was my finger from my attempts to hold the flame with the lighter.

Once I realized this wasn't going to happen, I thought the universe was probably laughing at me. Poor little shy, quiet girl failed again! I was a complete failure and that failed attempt only fueled my decline into darkness. A new level of darkness was upon me and it was only going to get worse. This night marked its birth and it would be another three years before it was all said and done.

Is this the part where I tell you what a failure you are? Your attempt was actually pretty damn funny, you spineless piece of trash. How hard could it be to light a shirt on fire!! You are worthless, always have been, always will be. I bet you're kicking yourself right now for letting me come out and comment on the sad state of your meaningless high school life. Trust me folks, she was ugly, she was a joke, she was a waste

of space. The best thing she could have done was kill herself, the thing is no one would have missed her. Her life was that useless.

Journal Excerpt:
High School Senior Year
May 8, 1989

> *"I lit my t-shirt on fire and let it burn for awhile while I was wearing it. We went back in and Jeff started watching the Metallica video. Elisa & Tony were on Elisa's waterbed in the dark I was sitting there ready to go home so I told them I was leaving and I headed for the door and sat in front of it with my jean jacket over my head. Soon Tony came out and pulled my jean jacket off my head and then I put it back on my head. Elisa came soon after that, pulled my jacket off and she wanted to know what was wrong. I told her I couldn't tell her because Tony & Jeff were there. I put my jacket back on my head and then Elisa pulled it off. We did this for a few minutes and she asked me to tell her what was wrong and that's when I started crying. Elisa wanted to know but I couldn't tell her not while Tony was there. She left me alone and then we all left to take me home.*

> *I couldn't tell Elisa what was wrong because it hurt too much. How do you tell your best friend that you like their boyfriend? I wrote Elisa, it was the only way. What I had done was wrong and it was mean. I can't believe I let myself like Tony a lot. I realize that I have to forget Tony and not go out with Elisa & Tony together for awhile until I get things straightened out with myself when I get straightened out then we can get together again like before. I didn't want to let Elisa know I started liking Tony because I didn't want to lose Elisa as my friend."*

After this incident, Elisa and Tony remained my friends. It was uncomfortable for a little while with Elisa, but she understood the whole situation. Things were all patched up but they were the only two people who saw the glimmers of the girl caught in the darkness needing help. Unfortunately for them and myself I didn't show too much of my hurt. Everything I had been through in high school was compounded over and over and then off to college I went.

CHAPTER THREE

"Ain't Too Funny When You'd Rather Die" – Rory Gallagher

My freshman year at Caledonia State College was a chance for me to start over. Or so I thought. Here I was with a chance for a new beginning because no one knew me. No one knew of my depression, so I had a chance to not be categorized and abused like I was in high school. How very wrong I was. The outside might have been different but the inside of me was still hurting. There was no clear picture of when it would stop or when the suffering would just go away.

In the first month of college I turned eighteen, had to get used to having a roommate, asked two guys out and both of them turned me down. When I finally did land a guy, my very first boyfriend, it only lasted three weeks. Turns out he was happy we broke up only because that meant he could date this sixteen year old from the nearby school. For me, we broke up because I couldn't handle him being around me all the time. I'm an only child so I'm not used to having someone around me twenty-four-seven, I felt claustrophobic. I needed my space. Also, some other guy was on my mind, someone from high school and finally, it was the first time I had alcohol.

That first year in college, these rejections made things worse. The feelings of loneliness and worthlessness just increased: every day something else was added to the darkness that was consuming me. I did freak out my roommate Amber Fuller to the point that she called home to ask her mother what to do about me. My first day at Caledonia I wrote a poem. One that I had left on my desk and how Amber saw it I don't know. For your reading pleasure, that poem is on the next page. It was written August 28, 1989.

All the negative thoughts from high school came with me to college and grew threefold.

The desire for someone to see me instead of being the invisible girl, someone to hold me, someone to care about me were compounded as were the thoughts of being ugly, not worthy and people not liking me. Self acceptance was an unknown concept to me. Every positive became a negative. "You look great!" translated into "You look horrible." Compliments were uncharted territory for me. I didn't know how to accept a compliment because all my life all I ever experienced was a barrage of insults. Even when teachers complimented me I didn't believe them. I never believed anyone was ever telling me the truth.

To Whom It May Concern: The Final Letter

I am a suicidal,
A veteran of the wrongful death.
I plan to create a big mess.
Time I plan for my trip,
Through my Standard window
I will make the final flip.
Down I fall to grass below
R.A.'s yelling "Oh My God, Oh No."
My open head, my blood makes grass grow.
Broken bones and a shattered mind,
Perfect moment, place and time,
Now the ground will be forever mine.

---

*I would like to properly introduce myself; I am the inner voice. I am Inner Me. Think of me as a crying little girl, just a child. Helpless and vulnerable, all I know is hurt. Even though I hurt, the outer part of me, the face shown to the world does not listen to me all the time. Well, more like the brain doesn't listen. From a young age we have had to rely on ourselves with no map, no sense of direction, not much of anything to guide us in this world. It was a confusing time, an overwhelming time with all the change going on. I was often ignored by the brain. While I was trying any way I could to keep us alive, the brain had other ideas. It was in full control of finding a way to die. Imagine yourself as a giant puzzle, pieces everywhere, a fragmented mess really and someway, somehow you have to put these pieces together. Imagine how frustrating that can be to keep trying to get pieces to fit but they just don't. Imagine doing that everyday, trying a new piece in the hopes it would click with another piece. I barely got to speak except in drunken fits and even then the brain censored me. I was pushed back and buried. The brain ignored everything I was telling it. It was in cahoots with the **Saboteur.** They tag teamed me in the worst way. I was the little girl lost in a big dark swamp.*

Yeah, you were drowning, choking all to pieces and you were a laugh. If you haven't figured it out yet boys and girls I'm the Saboteur, the Critic, I'm Miss Negativity! Every insult, criticism, you name it. If it

was negative I sucked it right up and replayed it over and over. The brain and I had a blast playing back every pitiful, painful incident. To be honest we just loved making the kid cry. We abused her just like everyone else. Poor kid just didn't know how to defend herself, not even against me. Oh, she was trying that's for sure, but she was getting the bad end of the deal. Sure, every now and then I'd let her think she was getting better and then just yank the rug from under her and watch her fall some more. I sort of miss the old days of berating her but I have to give the girl credit, she can at least fight me these days.

*The **Saboteur** and the brain never knew what I was really up to. Like I said I was trying any way I could to get her help. Trying to find some way for us to survive and the one thing that worked was music. She didn't realize at the time that music was healing her, helping her get through the really bad days. She loved music, I loved music and I knew it was probably the only way for us to survive, or at least keep us somewhat stable. Every attempt she made on her life, our life really, music was always playing in the background for the most part. In the tug of war of life and death, music was on the life side, pulling as hard as it possibly could.*

She was not consciously aware that music was healing her – us, but it wasn't happening in big chucks; it was small steps, steps that were nearly invisible. It wasn't until recently that she discovered just how important music was to her back then and how much it is to her now. But I'll talk about that later.

College was an interesting time. There was plenty of turmoil while I was there, but my freshman year paled in comparison to what was coming down the road. Sure, I had asked guys out and got rejected, had my first boyfriend which was a disaster, alcohol entered my life, along with more rejections and insults, and I had suitemates who look liked they just came from the Miss USA pageant. It was just a mess. However, little did I know that after having attempted two suicides in my life that five more were on their way.

Oh, as for the two guys I asked out who turned me down, there was a good reason for them to do so. It wasn't until a couple of years later that I learned they were gay. As a matter of fact they ended up dating each other and have been together for the past sixteen years. To this very day I'm still friends with both of them.

CHAPTER FOUR

"Strait Jacket Memories, Sedative Highs" – Queensryche

College was a giant dysfunctional soap opera for me. It was high school all over again. It was downright impossible to break free and find myself; to be authentic. There were times when I thought I was happy, that I was authentic but it was not to be. In college I just went with the flow, I was numb. There were two sides to me, and as much as I hurt, as much as I wanted to die, not all of my friends knew how bad off I was. I guess you could say I had selective sharing. Some of my friends knew I was an emotional train wreck but even they weren't sure to the extent. None of them knew I tried to light myself on fire in high school. All anyone really saw was me having crying fits when I drank too much. Alcohol and I just didn't mix, and it was during those nights of excessive drinking that my pain really showed itself.

Alcohol is a really good sedative and I sure drank my fair share of it in college. Well, actually alcohol is a bad sedative. You do stupid things when you have too much. I was one of those people constantly doing stupid things, like trying to kill myself. My choice of beverage was Popov Vodka, usually half a bottle followed by a Tylenol chaser. That's when I'd really be messed up. Sometimes it was vodka and a roof top or vodka and a knife across my wrists. Vodka was my favorite choice but beer was also prominent in my drinking days. I can't recall each and every suicide attempt; some stick with me more than others. I do remember, although it's a bit fuzzy, a time when I drank so much, took some pills and ended up in bed with a friend at my bedside, my friend Patrick Allen from Connecticut. He was so upset with me because like all the other people in my life, no one understood the destructive force that was going on inside me. Everyone saw glimmers, just bits and pieces, and thought they understood where I was coming from but they didn't. I remember Patrick at my bedside in my dorm room. He was upset to the point of crying and told me he couldn't look at me. He ended up leaving

15

me alone in my room, in my bed feeling the one thing I didn't want to feel anymore – rejected.

1/30/1990

Suicidal Me Returns

**Just when things
were going my way,
A bolt of lightning
struck my heart.
The suicidal me
is coming back again
and I see the knife,
the lighter and the roof
that I tried to use before.
I cry to get rid of the pain,
but it's stuck in my throat.
So many people to help me
but the pain still lingers.
I am embraced by miracle arms
but the pain is still here.
My teddy bear all wet
from my tears,
time for me to rest
upon a best friends chest,
To let the pain
fade away into nothing.**

That is the sick twisted game Patrick played with me. I liked Patrick a lot and we hung out and got close but not to the point of girl-friend/boyfriend. We were more like brother and sister. Patrick had a girl back home and for someone who was trying to be faithful to the one he loved, he didn't do a very good job of it. Our friendship was on and off. It was off for a long time when he started smoking a lot of pot. I wanted no part of that. He became a total burnout and I left him for dead, which is kind of how he left me. Eventually we came back around to each other. By the time he left Caledonia we were friends but I never heard from him after he left. My friendship with Patrick was probably the most dysfunctional friendship I ever had. More dysfunctional than the one with Michael, which some would say seems impossible, but it's true. What is it with guys from Connecticut?

You know, I did my best to derail this train but no amount of damage I could do could compare to the mental crap Patrick did. One

day he would hold her, give her hugs, cuddle to watch TV, chill out in his room to listen to Rush and then next thing you know he wants nothing to do with her. She was weak and convenient for him. He played her big time. For once I didn't have to do all the work, I just had to sit back and watch this unfold. Friends, not friends, friends, not friends, friends again; those two were just nuts. He hurt her probably more than Michael ever did, even though Michael hurt her pretty damn well. Patrick obviously was the one who did the most damage.

It's hard not drinking while in college because it seems everyone does it. After a while I cut back on my drinking because I would get chest pains from drinking vodka. It would feel like someone was sitting on my chest. So I basically quit the vodka and went to beer but I'd come back to vodka every once in a great while. I wasn't a party animal per say but I was a social drinker, hanging out with friends, kicking back and watching a few movies.

I had two sets of friends in college. The good group did all the fun stuff students do. We ate together, went to performances at the theatre, hung out in the TV room, and played pool. Most importantly, we laughed a lot. Then there was the bad group. They drank, smoked cigarettes, some of them smoked pot (although drug experimentation came much later for me) and stole pink flamingos from people's yards. They were the delinquents, the ones who had no cares at all. College was just one big playground to them.

Now being that I had these two sets of friends made life a little interesting. The good group disapproves of me hanging out with the bad group and the bad group disapproves of me hanging out with the good group. What to do, what to do? I just wanted to be friends with everybody – somebody. I was trying to find a group of people or just one person who was willing to accept me for who I was, but then again I didn't know who I was. Kind of hard to have one accept you if you haven't the slightest idea who you are. Honestly, how many college students know who they are? College is just another place where we are pressured by our peers to fit in. It's just a glorified version of high school with all of the cliques firmly present. The one difference is that in college you sometimes end up having a tormenter as your roommate or one of your suitemates. Then again, you sometimes are the witness to your roommate being tormented by someone else. Cruel as it is to say, it's sometimes nice to see others get kicked around because for once it's not you.

CHAPTER FIVE

"Bringin' On The Heartbreak" – Def Leppard

I suppose now would be a good time to talk about my track record with guys. A very pitiful record, I must say. In high school it seemed everyone I knew had a boyfriend except me. I suppose I put the pressure on myself that in order to be seen as normal I needed one too. Somehow I thought having a boyfriend would magically make all the bad stuff go away. The truth of the matter is I became obsessed with trying to get a boyfriend and in doing so, I really ruined my chances of meeting anyone.

> *Journal Excerpt:*
> *High School Senior Year*
> *February 27, 1989*
>
> **"I'm trying to make myself prettier so guys will notice me and that I might get a boyfriend because I want one very much. Yeah – I heard it before – having a boyfriend is not everything and don't worry about it. This is different.**
>
> **I need one to fill my empty space. For years I've had this space inside of me waiting to be filled by the love and joy of having a boyfriend. I haven't been on a date and that's pretty bad. I'll just have to stick it out I guess."**

My first semester at college was a nightmare on the guy front. I had so many crushes. I was desperate to have a boyfriend just to feel normal. I wanted to be like all the other girls because if someone like me had a boyfriend than I wasn't so bad after all. In the first semester at Caledonia I must have tried to hook up with at least six guys. One of them I did actually end up going out with, short lived as it was. From there my obsession to have a boyfriend got worse. It's like a part of me needed to have a boyfriend in order to feel worthy, accepted and most of all loved.

I guess that was the problem. I equated having a boyfriend to making my pain go away. A boyfriend would make me feel worthy and needed. If someone cared for me, then I was no longer the invisible girl. What I hungered for most was to be needed and feel loved. For the longest time I felt unloved and unworthy and even now, so many years after college, part of that feeling is still with me.

I really have no concept of love for I've never really experienced that blissful feeling people speak of. I've never experienced that magic moment before your first kiss like in the movies. To be honest, I can't really recall my first kiss. That's how uneventful it was, which is a shame because it should have been a magical moment, or so I thought.

I did have another boyfriend in college, but that lasted all of six months and was a disaster waiting to happen. Don't get me wrong, I enjoyed being with Don Firestone but in the end as I had sort of expected he was just killing time.

You see a friend of his was interested in my suitemate Natalie at the time. Turns out Don was interested in her as well and was waiting to see if anything would happen between her and his friend. When nothing did, well, you can guess what happened to me. Mind you it was a mutual break-up because I didn't know about the Natalie thing until after we broke up. Don wanted to break-up with me because I wasn't spending enough time with him. He was upset that I would pencil aside time to spend with him in my daily planner. The thing was, I was on academic probation and couldn't afford to flunk out of school. My concentration had to be on my studies and for whatever reason he couldn't grasp that. He couldn't grasp that school had to come first and so we broke up. He cried about it, I didn't. I knew it was going to happen before it actually did and next thing I know he's off running around campus with Natalie.

There were plenty of guys I got close to but ended up being just friends with. The list is just too long to write out. That basically sums me up really, always the friend never the girlfriend. What was worse was finding out later from certain guys that would have dated me but (1) they were to shy to say anything or (2) they would have asked me out but didn't like my friends. Slightly messed up I know. I hated the words "just friends" as it was all I ever heard.

There were the guys who feasted on my emotions, sensed I was messed up and played me for as long as they could. A good example of that was Andy Anderson. Andy was from Massachusetts and a member of the Kappa Delta Phi fraternity. He was a nice guy but he was a major flirt and I fell for his spell. We would hang out, kiss a lot, and lay in my bed taking naps. Pretty harmless stuff but when I tried to hold his hand one night while

> *Journal Excerpt:*
> *CSC Freshman Year*
> *September 4, 1989*
>
> *"...yeah friends, that's all I ever am to a guy, a friend. I'm sick of being a guy's friend. I want to be their girlfriend. I just want to be held, to have someone care about me, I want to feel like I'm wanted. I don't mind being friends with a guy but that's as far as I ever get. I'm a freshman in college and I haven't had some guy like me more than a friend. Why can't I be like this gorgeous girl that you find in a magazine or something. Why can't I be the girl who gets the guys? I realize that it is hard to find a guy who is caring, a little romantic, semi-intelligent, understanding, one who won't push you away and will always be there when you need them."*

walking across campus, he shook me off. Then the information that he had a girl back in Massachusetts came forth. That upset me for obvious reasons and from there I went back to my dorm without him. One of his sorority sisters, Trisha Patterson, knew him and I were not dating but hanging out a lot and when she spotted me crying she wanted to know what was going on, so I told her. She was ticked.

Later I learned that Trisha laid into him pretty darn well and the rest of the sorority sisters weren't too happy with him either. Score one for me.

While Andy disappeared from Caledonia for a year or so, he eventually returned and we sort of picked up where things left off. However, there was at least one part of Andy that he rarely showed and that was how much he was willing to take care of me. See, the Kappa brothers always threw this yearly party at Halloween called 'Spooks 'N' Spirits' where everyone just goes to this large field with a giant tent, music and all the alcohol you could imagine. The year Andy returned to school I was more stable than I had been and had cut back on the alcohol intake but I didn't trust myself. Andy had to work the party but he told me if I didn't feel good or thought I may have a breakdown to come find him. I did end up finding him because I didn't think I could trust myself after having several mixed drinks. I was drunk but not stumbling, mumbling "where the hell am I" drunk. I was somewhat coherent and I remember Andy taking me back to the Kappa house but I was almost a prisoner as he wouldn't let me out of his room to hang out with the other people at the house.

I ended up spending the night with him, but nothing happened. We watched TV and then fell asleep, that was it. In the morning he gave me a ride back to campus. It was like we were trying to rekindle something but in the end I found strength and walked away from him. He was toxic. You'd think I would learn to stay away from the fraternity guys but oh no, I had to try again!

Andy was like Patrick. He really did a number on her. Blasted idiot. Folks, you should have been there to witness this pathetic display. Please. She thought her and Andy would be boyfriend and girlfriend. HA HA HA! So desperate to have a guy, so desperate she was. What guy was going to go out with her anyway? She was overweight, ugly, shy and just a piece of yuck. White trash at its best. What a loser.

*Hey, lay off. True, we were desperate but only because we were lonely, fragile and desperately needed to feel safe and wanted. There's nothing wrong with wanting someone to hold us, to comfort us. You're so damn critical of everything but let's be honest **Saboteur,** even you need love.*

Please keep in mind that when I went to Caledonia the on campus population was about a thousand students. Everyone pretty much knew everyone else. I knew a lot of Kappa brothers and sisters as well as Sigma Psi brothers and sisters. I casually knew a lot of people in both organizations and had made some great friends, too. Andy, for all his little quirks, was an okay guy if not a bit creepy at times. His opposite was a guy named David Smythe who was part of the Sigma Psi fraternity.

David, Andy and I all worked at the college radio station. I met a lot of people on campus while working there. Anyway, David and I slowly became friends. He was incredibly good looking and actually wanted to know how I was. Perhaps he could sense that I was a bit fragile because he was always so kind and gentle with me.

He'd ask me for favors or I'd help him with something at the radio station, he was just a cool guy and yes, I had a crush on him. Strangely enough, I didn't want to date him. I really enjoyed his company and I think it was because he treated me with kindness and didn't try to walk all over me.

Whenever I helped him, he would do something nice for me in return. I never asked him to do nice things for me but he would anyway and maybe that's where my generous nature sprang from.

College was a rollercoaster when it came to guys. Eventually I learned that having a boyfriend was not a major life priority. As a matter of fact, I don't place much emphasis on having a boyfriend these days. Hell, I don't ever plan to marry because to be honest, I think marriage is overrated. Yes, I'm lonely but to be honest after all these years having a boyfriend isn't important but being with a guy is to an extent. These days I just want a guy who I can get a hug from anytime I need one, a guy I can walk down the street with arm and arm looking at store windows, a guy I can sit on a park bench with and watch a sunset, a guy I can hang out with at a small cafe writing in my journal while he reads a book or something, a guy I can snuggle up with on a couch to watch a movie, a guy that I can reveal my inner self to. Sounds like a romantic fantasy that can't happen but you know, I think there is such a guy out there. I don't want a boyfriend. I'm just looking for a friend boy. A guy I can be close to and just enjoy the journey of life with.

You could say that not only was I wanting to fill the dark space inside me but wanting desperately to feel and have something that everyone else had around me – love. I sometimes think love is non-existent even though it's all around me. To all the people who know love, you're lucky. Maybe one day I'll find out for myself just how wonderful it may be.

After all these years, the ache for love is still here. It is a concept that I struggle to bring to life. How can one receive the gift of love from someone if there is no basis, no example to go by? Michael gave us a glimpse with unconditional love but it took many years to understand it, and even now the concept gives me trouble. When it comes to love I cry because I see it all around and yet have never felt it myself. We – all the parts that make us a person - have never experienced such a beautiful gift. When you come from an unaffectionate family, how do you then create what affection is if the people you build yourself from don't provide it to you?

The concept of caring for another is not wasted, I understand this. I understand compassion and sorrow but love is a concept I can't make us understand fully. It's a vicious circle because people often say that love will only come your way if you learn to love yourself but how can someone love themselves if they do not have a template to help them understand? I feel that I have failed in providing such a basic emotion as love, the feeling of it. I know that I wish to feel it, to feel the pure emotion, the joy that comes with such a thing. It is one thing to accept oneself, it is another to love oneself. Acceptance and love are not the same thing.

CHAPTER SIX

"Don't Cry" – Seal

I've certainly done my fair share of crying since high school and still do to this day. Almost everyday I go home and just sit and cry for a little while. I've been carrying around so much emotional baggage that I need to empty bits and pieces of it now and then. I have good and bad days and on the bad days I feel like falling to my knees and crying as hard as I possibly can. You know those women you see on the news during a major catastrophe that are on their knees crying, wailing in pain as someone holds them, equally crying but trying to comfort the person who is hurting the most? That's me, I'm that woman sometimes. Crying like I just lost a loved one but in my case I'm crying because....I guess I'm still mourning. I should have stopped years ago but I haven't. I mourn the loss of myself or maybe I mourn the fact that I found myself. I'm not sure. I know I mourn for the loss of friends but I mourn the loss of strangers, too. I mourn for a loss that I cannot really describe. Perhaps I mourn because I no longer wish to die for that part of me has died – sort of. That part of me is at rest even though it remains close by and could be resurrected at any time. All it will take is a series of dark events to send me back to a place I never want to visit again. A friend of mine once said that ninety-nine percent of the time you force yourself to be happy and the other one percent of the time when no one is looking you cry. These days, I'm fifty-fifty, but there used to be a time when I cried ninety-nine percent of the time.

There are so many unresolved issues from our suicidal swamp that even I don't know where to begin. While that part of us is buried, it doesn't mean it's dead. Those dark years are important to reflect on and to learn and grow from, although attempting to reflect on it all at once is a big mistake. There's too much to look at and examine, it definitely needs to be done in pieces.

As I stated earlier I'm like a crying little girl and that is what I am referenced as. If I had to pick an age, I'd be sixteen, although part of me is very much like a little girl about eight. For many years that's all I did, just cry and cry and hurt. I was very hurt for a long time and then with the help of Michael, healing began and I don't cry as much as I used to. I live in beautiful little house that resides in the middle of a beautiful meadow.

There is but one tree, a mighty Oak and a nice cliff with a view of the ocean. There is an old, wooden fence that runs across the meadow about a hundred feet from the house. It is a beautiful place although it used to be a bit dark. I used to be in the meadow all the time but I've been living in the house for quite some time now as it's very cozy. On the other side of the fence is a dark meadow. No green grass, no flowers, nothing is alive. Everything is very dead. I used to live on that side of the fence. It's where I did the majority of my crying. While I do live in the house most days, I do come out and sit on the fence, balancing the dark and the light. The external part of us, the side of us that's shown to the world day in and out sits on the fence, too.

It's all we know where to be. Happiness is still new to us and so sitting on the fence is the best we can do. I do tend to live in the house a lot, but it's not like I'm being locked away.

While the house is beautiful to be in, and is warm and welcoming, it still needs a bit of repair to make it stable. Love has not found its way to this house. There is room for it, but I am still sorting through all the baggage from years past, trying to ditch what I no longer need in order to make room for nicer things.

Seven years of depression and four years of suicide attempts will never vanish from me. It is part of who we are, it's part of our very core. It's who I am and it's who she is and even the **Saboteur** *will agree it's who it is. This is who we are collectively. We are a survivor, we are a suicide survivor. We have dodged death several times, fighting our way through the darkened swamplands to find a place of peace. Not perfect peace but just peace, a calm in the storm winds. There will always be a dark place for us, it will never go away and at times we visit it but don't relive it. Darkness does call to us now and then. We are ever fearful that it will grab us, torment us and bring us back to the meadow of death. Dragging us to a place we never want to visit again. Every day is a battle to stay on this side of the fence, the side of the beautiful meadow and the bluest of skies.*

Cry, cry, cry....what a baby! It's sad and pitiful to cry so much but even I know the pain that was felt. We all feel it and can't escape it. It's messed up. Blowing things out of proportion is my job and compounding the pain that comes with it. I helped drive us to the darkened swamplands, the twisted forest of cerebral nightmares. I love death, but as much as death appeals to me, all I know is that I hate it when she

cries. **Crying is weak and for the monster that I am every time that little bitch comes crying along I just want to demolish her. I can't help it folks, when she starts to cry and the thoughts of negativity begin to flow I have to add to it. It's my job to help destroy her even though doing so would consequently kill me, too. I guess I'm just a sick twisted individual. I'm called the Saboteur for a reason, folks, it's my job to seek and destroy.**

You're such a bully. Shut up! Seek and destroy? That's mighty rich of you to say you self-loathing bastard. We're in this together whether you like it or not. You're just upset because for once, she's in control and keeping you in check. You're upset that all the tools she's picked up over the years are working. Music heals and you hate the fact that it does. They say music soothes the savage beast so get used to it!

CHAPTER SEVEN

"It's Such A Magical Mysteria" – Def Leppard

Music has always been an important part of my life. In high school you could name a song and I could tell you what album it was from and if the song was on side A or B of the vinyl record. Damn, I miss vinyl records. The sound of the snap crackle as the record would spin on the turntable and the cover art always rocked. I just love music. I listen to music as much as I can and honestly I think I'd die without it.

I never really understood the importance of music until recently. Ever since I was old enough to listen to music, I was always drawn to certain bands and more importantly guitar players. After all these years there is one guitar player who has always stayed with me. He was my favorite when I was sixteen and he's my favorite at thirty-six. His name is Steve Clark and he was one of the co-lead guitarists in Def Leppard. I started listening to Def Leppard in my teens; they were part of my foundation, my survival. I just didn't know it at the time.

I recently dusted off my Leppard albums because I was working on another writing project that triggered a memory in me and so it began this trip down memory lane. Past reminders from a forgotten time in my life started to stir.

As soon as the guitar lines in any Def Leppard song before 1989 kick up I hear Steve Clark's magical note dances. I have always believed that I hear an additional tune when listening to any number of Def Leppard songs. The tune is buried under the main guitar lines. It's a faint tune that only seems to come to life when I'm creatively working on something or writing. My ears have tuned into Steve's guitar riffs over the years and from those notes I swear he's playing an additional song on top of the one he's actually playing. So if he's cranking out Hysteria, I seem to hear another guitar line besides the one being played by co-lead guitarist Phil Collen. It's like Steve stuck in some additional notes.

As I listen to CDs, dig out my buried Def Leppard paraphernalia – which for some reason I never threw out – and go to websites to read about Steve, my past comes back clearly. As I read old articles about Steve, I feel like I'm reading about myself. He was a likable person with a sense of humor, who was depressed, alcoholic and shy. He was a tormented soul, lost in a world he didn't know how to survive in.

Sounds so much like me in years past. The only difference between me and Steve was that he was earning millions of dollars a year, playing in a band in front of millions of people, recording albums and doing the one thing he loved, playing guitar. I never really wanted to be a rock star, but I dreamed long ago of playing the guitar like him or any number of the guitar gods I admired in my youth. I wanted to make records, to handle the technical end of the music business, but the closest I came was being a radio announcer for eight years.

Lately, I have been working on understanding myself and my relationship to Michael. I question if I really have escaped depression's grasp or if I've just been fooling myself for the past fifteen years.

Perhaps this is the reason the triggered memories of my past have come to the forefront. The answer that I have been seeking might be with Steve, reminding me that while it was comforting to know that someone else was suffering like me half way around the world, there was an unspoken understanding – a validation of some sort. In Steve's guitar playing, the Riffmaster himself was revealing his pain not in words but in musical notes, a pain that I could identify with. A reminder that I wasn't alone after all, I suppose. That out there in this giant world someone understood what I was going through. It's funny to think that because Steve Clark never met me and I never met him, yet I knew him. Even now when I think of his music, I acknowledge him and yet acknowledge something in myself.

I'm not the depressed fragile girl I once was as I haven't tried to kill myself in fifteen years. The alcohol is behind me as I haven't had a drink in years. Steve Clark didn't survive his alcoholism or his loneliness but I did. I don't always give myself credit for making it this far in life. My life could have ended years ago if I had succeeded on any number of my alcohol-fueled, pill popping excursions. As much as I wanted to die I guess a bigger part of me, a part I didn't understand at the time wanted to live. Maybe that's the Steve Clark mystery tune I hear, a painful song about finding oneself.

I see so much of myself in Steve and the similarities of our lives as confirmation from a famous person that it's okay to be down, to be depressed, to drink in excess and to take a few pills. Not that drinking and taking pills is a good thing, but when you are hitting the bottle yourself and popping a few pills now and then to end the pain, the hell you're in, looking up to see your Guitar God doing practically the same thing and feeling pain like you, you feel good about that. Kind of like, well if he's doing it and feels that way then it must be okay if I do it and feel this way.

Steve Clark has been dead for sixteen years now and yet, he's like the crying child in me, and he's never left. Steve Clark is someone that a few of us met, some of us watched in awe or simply knew by the music he made. To some he is a friend long gone. To others he is a friend who never left. He made more people laugh and smile than he did angry and sad. He was a son, a brother, a band mate, a guitar player, a musical muse, a friend to us all. He left behind a musical legacy that cannot be touched or matched by another guitar player. His was a type of music that touched us all. When he played his guitar it spoke to all of us, it touched us all in a very intimate way. With heart and soul he played and to us he showed himself. He showed the glorious light of his spirit when he played his guitar, a gift not many know how to share. He left behind a tremendous gift, the gift of music. What we heard from him yesterday can still be heard today and we'll hear it again tomorrow. His music will never die as long as we remember and honor him.

The music he created hasn't died for it sits inside me. Every Def Leppard song that he contributed to moves me on some level. Physically Steve Clark is dead but he's very much alive in me. Just because you're dead doesn't mean you're gone.

So to Mr. Clark, I must give thanks for he inspired me in so many ways to become a better person.

The painful notes he played actually kept him alive because playing guitar was the one thing he loved. His notes are filled with the sounds of pain, struggle, joy, anger, strength and brief moments of beautiful peace. Somehow I must have maneuvered my way to find the joy and peace in the music way back when.

What's that bible line? Something about walking through the valley of the shadow of death, I will fear no evil for you are with me. I can't remember it exactly but maybe that's what the gift of music can do. Perhaps the key to surviving is to tune into our own inner song. In my case, it was an outer song which I tuned into. It was Steve Clark's inner song. Maybe some of us need to hear an outer song that somehow triggers us to find our inner song and it's that tune which helps you walk through the valley instead of becoming a permanent resident.

A part of me wants to light a candle in honor of everyone whose musical tune whether outer or inner I've heard and borrowed notes from to make my own inner song stronger. Maybe I'm not so far off comparing Steve Clark's life to a song; maybe I'm not so far off comparing my own life to a song. Gosh, I could write about Steve Clark forever. My brain rambles on the Steve Clark track at the moment as it would seem that indeed my survival was due to music – his music.

Steve Clark for whatever reason is my Guitar God, even though I don't play the guitar. His masterful melodic tones swept me to a place that touched my soul, my core, my being. It is true that for all the hardship in my young life, I made it through due to a complex combination of notes strung together to make a soaring song that touched my spirit. As I look back on my dark years, Steve Clark gave me strength. He shared some invisible power to fight through and not give up on myself. Things were never easy but in the song of a stranger I found a way to keep going. In the sounds of Def Leppard as a whole group, I found a way to keep going. They showed me that no matter what life throws at you, that you just have to keep trying. It would have been easy for them to give up after drummer Rick Allen lost his arm in a car accident or Steve's untimely death but they didn't. They forged together, ever stronger than the days and years before and solidified themselves as brothers and as a band.

Steve Clark meant more to me than I knew back then. Only now do I realize that he meant so much to my fragile little being and that any attack on him was like an attack on me. He was my role model I suppose, a giant among guitar players in my tormented life who somehow gave me hope and the strength to keep fighting, even when I didn't think I wanted to live anymore.

I wish I could tell Steve "thank-you" for letting me hear his eternal song of hope, that even when we are at our weakest, our darkest, there is always a light inside us that sings. I never got to meet Steve Clark in person but it doesn't seem to matter even after all these years. His song remains inside me, forever playing its melodic riff of truth, filling me up and guiding me with an inner peace I had long since forgotten I knew.

Maybe there is something to be said about Psalm 23 and walking through the valley of the shadow of death. For me and what I've been through it's a nod to the music of Steve Clark, of Def Leppard at a time in my life when I was walking in the shadow of death.

They helped me through it so that I would fear no evil because they were with me. Because of the frequency of their song, their tune was heard by my ears, my soul and that gave me my strength to continue on.

To walk through the valley of death and survive that walk is a big deal. I walked through the valley alone but music was my guide. Those of us who are viewed as weak are actually the strongest. We have walked a path many don't know or understand.

Some of us make this great journey through the darkness and survive while a few of us don't. I do not see those who don't make it as weak because most of them tried to make it through the pain, the sorrow and the darkness that surrounded them. Some may have given up because it was too much, but a few fight their way to a better place.

For those that don't make the journey through the valley, I hope they understand that by just trying they have given hope to the rest of us on the same journey. It is a shared darkness, a shared sorrow, a shared view of death and we are never truly alone in the valley for there are many around us who feel the same way. All of us together are on a journey to get to greener pastures and to be better than who we were.

It strikes me that maybe, just maybe Steve Clark's guitar lines resonate with me so deeply, strumming my soul, because we were walking through the valley together at the same time. It's a strange concept that my little mind has put together. If we are truly never alone and all of us are connected to each other in some way, then it's plausible that Steve and I were indeed walking together through the valley of the shadow of death at the same time.

Maybe my connection to certain musicians, actors and sports figures isn't so much of what they do for an occupation but some unspoken language that resonates from them, an unspoken language that we have all forgotten to know how to hear. The inner and outer songs I wrote about earlier might actually be just one song and that when I tune into someone else's song which resonates with mine a connection is made. Maybe each one of us is carrying a part of the same song. Maybe someone carries the melody. Perhaps someone has part of the harmony, someone carries the actual notes, and someone out there has the words. Maybe the reason for Steve Clark and Def Leppard having such a profound meaning on my life is because they have parts of the universal song, my internal song.

There has to be some sort of structure to this. Well, there doesn't have to be but my Virgo mind says there should be. Music has always been a large part of my life, it is my survival tool. If I didn't have music I'd go nuts. As I said, my mind has come up with this universal song theory and I'm not sure if I'm on to something or not. All I know is my song isn't ready to end yet; if anything, I'm still writing it.

Steve Clark influenced me and I looked up to him. I found comfort in him and maybe knowing that he was walking through the same dark valley I was made me feel better. We are often comforted knowing someone is going through the same pain as we are. When I see pictures of Steve Clark my heart aches for him or maybe I ache for loss, which is what he represented to me. Perhaps he was a larger than life reflection of me.

They say Steve didn't commit suicide when he died, that it was an overdose of alcohol and pain medication for the three ribs he'd broken in a fall that did him in. Music for Steve was his refuge from the pain people inflicted on him and the pain he inflicted on himself. All it takes is one or more negative thoughts and a depressed person can runaway with those two and turn them into fifty.

I was reading that Steve's band mates always had to tell him that he was a good guitar player because he didn't think he was. They were constantly trying to reassure him that he was. Gee, sounds like someone I know – ME! What few friends I had back then and even friends I have now constantly remind me that I'm a good person.

If people are reflections of who we are on the inside, could Steve Clark be a reflection of me even though I never met him? Could Def Leppard be the reflection of family or more closely the reflection of what it would be like to have siblings?

I don't know. I just know that Steve Clark and Def Leppard deserve to be mentioned in my little story. To write about my journey and not include them seems – wrong. It seems disrespectful. For five guys who helped me so much, they deserve a lot more than two chapters in my book but it's all I can give them along with a great respect for who they are and what they have accomplished. I only hope that I can be that way to someone else. Maybe that's the whole point of writing my story in the hopes that someone else won't feel so out of place. That being inspired by a musician, a ballplayer, an actor, an artist or whoever, is a legitimate way of trying to survive, not something to be ashamed of which is how I used to feel. These days I know that my admiration, my respect for Steve, Def Leppard, and any number of people I'm drawn to is a beautiful gift from the universe. The universe helped me see these gifts and maybe it took me awhile to understand their importance but at least I understand them now. Death and destruction may go hand in hand but Death and reconstruction go together to – I should know. Thanks, Steve, for helping me to reconstruct myself.

CHAPTER EIGHT

"Rock of Ages" – Def Leppard

Ah, Def Leppard. Certainly brings me back to my youth, a youth I missed out on in some aspects because I was wasting away in depression. As I mentioned in the previous chapter, Steve Clark was important to me but so was the band he was in, Def Leppard. Def Leppard's line-up may be different now because Steve is dead and Vivian Campbell took his place but the spirit of who they are remains unchanged. Whatever magic Def Leppard possessed when I listened to them in my teenage and college years has never ever left them. I'm in my thirties now and I can still hear this amazing sound buried underneath every single one of their songs. It is strange to say this but my whole sense of what a supportive, caring family should be comes from them. I'm not sure how to explain that. I just know that when I see a picture of them or hear one of their songs I feel good about myself. I feel as though someone just came up to me and patted me on the shoulder or gave me this huge warm hug. I feel as though they are with me, encouraging me and being supportive of me in their own way. When I have a bad day, I listen to their music and I feel better after a while. Def Leppard has always been there when I needed them. They never yelled at me, put me down or tossed insults my way. When I needed to feel that someone cared about me, that someone did support me, my warped little mind convinced the fragile part of me that the guys did care about me. That they had a vested interest in making sure I was okay and safe. This of course, is a bit silly since I don't know them but it's amazing what the mind and body will do to help heal you when you're in pain. All these little mechanisms of coping with the pain I was feeling from my younger years have not left me. I still use them to this day. So yes, I will readily admit that on any given night in dreamland, a member of Def Leppard is helping me work something out.

It took you a while but you finally discovered how healing music was to us. It was the last thing I knew to do to keep us alive. If music didn't work I really don't know what else would have distracted you from the dark thoughts of killing yourself. In between your attempts was music, healing you bit by bit. You were not aware of my plan or how music was healing you. You were totally oblivious to what I was doing but it worked. You're here, I'm here, and we're alive. Do you realize that as a teenager Def Leppard was your favorite band and they're the only band that you still listen to today as intently as you did when you were younger? Haven't you ever wondered why? It's more than just Steve Clark, although he was part of it, but the music of Def Leppard has always resonated with you. When you feel bad, what have you always done after all these years?

You've turned on the radio or stuck in a CD. You listen to all types of music but most of all you put on Def Leppard. Why? Because listening to them makes you feel better, they always have. True, for a while you didn't listen to them because you didn't need to, but you're starting to again, because their music is the one thing that has always been with you. Def Leppard has always been there for you.

Through all your pain, through your attempts, bad relationships, good relationships, everything you have experienced in your life the one thing that has never judged you, never left you, never criticized you but supported you, been there when you needed it, is them – Def Leppard. They're the one constant that has been in your life from the beginning of your depression to now. Listening to them makes you feel better. Listening to them not only brings you back to your teenage years but you've grown as the band as grown. You know those posters that go "Everything I Learned About Life I Learned from..." Well for you, it would say "Everything I Learned About Life I Learned from Def Leppard." While it's not one hundred percent true it's at least sixty percent. They have been your template for a long time. They have inspired you in more ways than I can mention.

You almost feel like you know them but what you feel is the reminder. They have been with you through everything and look how far you have come. Look how far they have come, all that they have been through. That's why their music is still a part of your life because you've grown up with them just as they have grown up with you. They remind you that no matter how bad things get, you can't give up and that anything is possible.

I know I paint a somewhat rosy picture but I'm not trying to on purpose. What I'm trying to illuminate is that there are things in this world that you may never understand but know that the world does respond and answers you the only way it knows how. Repeatedly I have tried to beat into your head that you are not alone and I know you understand that but I also know that you wrestle with it. You have a hard time accepting the fact that you are not alone because you are alone.

For the record, Steve Clark serves a purpose which you already figured out. Now you wonder what purpose Vivian Campbell serves. Besides the fact that Vivian stepped into Steve's vacated role in Def Leppard, he's a representation of the next stage of your life. The part you're working on now. Confused? Let me explain to you. There was the Steve Clark era in Def Leppard and now there is the Vivian Campbell era. Steve was full of pain which you identified with and understood but now I'm using Vivian to help you with the stage you're in now. You have sort of picked up on it already. Things change and Vivian was the outsider; a new member of the family if you will. He's no longer a stranger or an outsider, but to a lot of people he was because he was seen as a replacement for Steve. Change can be traumatic to people. It took a while to welcome him into the family. Moving from Steve to Vivian was a transformation; pain was replaced with contentment. Vivian's purpose in helping us...mostly you really...is to touch a place of heritage. He's the good stuff. The bad stuff is behind us, and now it's time for the good things to come into our life. Vivian represents humor, he is a reminder of your own Irish roots, he plays the guitar and smiles a lot. He's another template showing you that good things can happen.

A kid from Belfast grows up to be accomplished guitar player. This is a template you've been shown before, but now it's been altered slightly. Steve's template and Vivian's template are similar, but while Steve had a darker aspect in his template, Vivian's is much brighter.

There are lots of templates of strength and goodness around you if you just look. I know I'm always looking which leads me to ask, why do you keep missing them? Open your eyes a bit more and listen to the music that sweeps into us; it's there for you to see and hear.

Template after template. Faith, Trust, Love, Happiness, Sadness, Anger, Death, Joy are all a part of life's little journey. You've already experienced the really bad stuff, now it's time for you to experience the really good stuff.

As for the people who don't get what you mean with all of this, screw them. It's not meant for them to understand, it's meant for you to understand. If they happen to understand, great! If not, their loss really because they're missing out on something wonderful. Music is a powerful gift from the universe and it's a shame that so many people ignore its healing qualities and the lessons of life it teaches.

CHAPTER NINE

"Is There Anybody Listening?" - *Queensryche*

As I trudged my way through college, I sent up the "I'm in trouble" sign a few times and yet once again, no one really noticed. My Head Resident, my Resident Assistant and a few friends sort of noticed but didn't do anything about it. Just like high school, I shot up the flares and no one came running.

Once again, the thoughts of "you're not worthy" were reinforced. Here I am hurting like hell, confused as can be, I don't know who I am or how to be and all I really want is for someone to see me. Someone to hold me and tell me it will all get better; to know that someone gives a shit about me. Maybe in high school and college we're not equipped to deal with these feelings or know how to help someone else in this scenario. I don't know. Being ignored adds fuel to the fire if you're depressed. Then again, pretty much anything said or done to you is just fuel to fire. Even if someone says something nice to you, it's just more fuel to the fire. As I wrote earlier, all that is positive becomes negative and you basically feel like crap. You start to believe you're crap and you live the life of crap. If you're crap, honestly why would you want to live? See what I mean? It's a very vicious cycle to get out of.

Take everything negative in nature anyone has ever said to you and multiply it by one hundred. Then imagine it being said over and over in your head, like a looped tape. This was what was going on in my brain, my own personal hell. If that imagery doesn't help, remember when you were a kid getting picked on? Imagine that group of kids constantly picking on you twenty-four hours a day, 365 days a year. Now do you understand? While that is going on in your head, throw in a bad self image. Seriously, you look in the mirror and you are disgusted with what you see because guess what? The kids who pick on you tell you you're ugly and that gets repeated over and over and you believe it. Now throw in the fact that people ignore you even when you do something that in most cases should get someone's attention but doesn't. You become a walking disaster and all you want is for the voices you hear to stop. All you want is for the smile on your face to be genuine. When some asks, "How are you?" you really want to be able to tell them you feel great. You want to be authentic in your responses but you can't when you are dealing with the above.

After a while you just start faking happiness. You think maybe it will kick in on its own any moment and this depressed suicidal life you have will just go away on its own. If only it was that easy. Writing about this is bumming me out but it needs to be said because people just don't get it. I have friends now who don't understand why someone would want to end their life, and to be honest I don't have the answers. It's different for each person. I had my reasons but they may not be the same reasons as to why someone else would try.

The only hope you have is that someone sees you or you find someone who touches you in a way that helps heal you a bit. I was fortunate to have that in college. Maybe that's why I miss college because when I needed someone to hold me, someone to hug me, someone to listen, I had a number of friends I could go to. Mind you it wasn't until my wake-up call that these types of people showed up, but better late than never, right? Well, I also had some other friends show up who were not of this world.

Yes, you read that correctly. I'm not even sure where to begin with this one, but I guess I can trace it back to one night in particular. I think it was the fall semester of my fifth year at CSC. Yes, I was on the five year plan. I actually flunked out of school (yet another warning sign) my third year and was put on academic probation, and I switched my concentration from TV to Radio. My parents had no clue about this back then, and to this day they still don't know I flunked out of school. When you're on probation you can make an appeal before they actually boot your ass out the door. In my case, I won my appeal so I was still able to go to school. I just needed to bring my grades up, which I did. So my academic probation was for year three and my appeal allowed me to stay for year four and by year five I was on good academic standing again. However, if it wasn't my grades trying to get me kicked out of school, it was something, or should I say someone, else.

In the fall of my final year at CSC, the Ouija board was the "in" thing in my dorm. Before I continue on, I should mention that I've always been interested in the paranormal, metaphysics, and new-age stuff. I should also note that there will be some religious themed beliefs that will pop up as I recount this. I simply ask that you keep your mind open and yes, it's okay if you read the following recount of events and think I'm nuts. Believe me, I thought I was.

Where was I? Oh yeah, the Ouija board. One night, I was invited to join some friends in a dorm room for a little fun. Mind you these people weren't exactly my friends, more like friendly acquaintances. You know that fuzzy place between friend and acquaintance – that's what they were. Anyway, I guess the planchette was moving pretty well until I entered the room. It came to a dead stop. I told everyone it was because I knew too much. Meaning I knew too much about the paranormal. Hard for a spirit to scare people when one can ruin your fun, know what I mean? I told them to ask the spirit and sure enough the spirit answered positively.

After this first encounter and a few others I went and got my own Ouija board. Then the fun really began. The first time with my Ouija board I was with my friends Jake Morris and Frank Warner. We got Lucifer. As I think about it now, it's kind of funny because we got Lucifer, Satan and all the other various names to call the guy. It was a strange night. Jake, Frank and I were rattled enough that we went for a late night walk around campus and just talked about stuff.

When I got back to the dorm, things got a little interesting to say the least. These days I'm not really rattled by unexplainable paranormal stuff. I think some of it's rather cool. Anyway, I said good night to Jake and Frank as they headed upstairs. The thing that freaked me out the most was when I went to my room to go to bed. I came into my suite and walked to my room. I noticed the light in the bathroom was turned off. I went into my room, turned on the lights, took my coat off and then I heard a "click." I walked out into the suite hallway and noticed the light in the bathroom was on.

I went into the bathroom and no one was in there – it was empty! Needless to say, I freaked out, turned off the lights and went to bed.

I'm not sure how the group of four came together exactly. I know it started with Raine Kubacheski and me using the board because both she and I had the same dark parts to our personalities. The mystery of the otherworld was intriguing to us. At this point, I knew Michael as we had already had the infamous walk and talk. Keira Collen and I had been friends for a couple of years by this point. I think all of us had an attraction to the undead and considering Michael looked liked Death, it made sense that the four of us would have some interesting nights in candlelight.

The first night Michael and Keira joined Raine and I wasn't the first night that the spirit we had reached asked that I channel. Something I was good at doing. The spirit we were in contact with was named BJ. He claimed to be a teenager who had been hit in the head with a camera which caused his death. Seems rather far fetched; seriously who ever died from being hit in the head with a camera? Anyway, he liked playing practical jokes and liked it when we laughed. I had always refused to channel when he asked but knowing that Michael was in the room, I agreed to give it a shot.

I had never done channeling but I knew what it was, remember I said I was into this paranormal stuff. Anyway, being that I had never done it before, BJ was kind enough to tell me to just relax. Turns out I can do it rather easily, a natural gift I suppose. Don't ask what was said because I don't re-member, as I went into a trance like state. I do remember how I felt after-wards; it was almost like a tiny bit of residue from BJ was still with me. I also felt totally relaxed and had the best night of sleep ever.

If there is one thing I like about channeling it's that amazing night of sleep afterwards. It's hard to explain what channeling is like. Think of leav-ing your physical body and standing behind it, looking at yourself and all that connects you to it is a string. Now imagine someone else standing next to you and filling up your physical body. You're still connected by the string but think of the other person just taking your place. It's the best I can do to describe it and it's the strangest of sensations to feel. For months, Raine, Keira, Michael and I used the board. We had fun and at the time, I think each of us needed it. At that moment in time we needed each other and that is what brought us together. All of us were on journeys to find ourselves and the board helped each one of us grow in some way or at least change the way we viewed the world. In one particular case, karmic debt was being paid off.

So blah, blah, blah about all this Ouija board stuff. After a while we moved on from BJ to someone with a bit more oomph – Death. Yup, we used to talk to Death. It was strange at first to be talking to Death, or Shadow as we affectionately called him. Usually, we called him "S" if we were talking about stuff and those not in our group were close by. To be honest, we called all the spirits we talked to by the letter of their name; in some cases all we were given was just a letter. People forget that our names are power and resonate who we are. So for a while we were conversing with Death and learning a few things about the "other side".

I got into it more than the others; I was at the college library reading about Archangels, Angels, Death and a whole slew of other things like auto-matic writing. This is something else I'm also good at which makes sense since I love to write. Automatic writing is such a cool thing and to be honest I don't do it the way most experts claim you're supposed to.

Then again, when have I ever done anything like I'm supposed to? Like most, I started out with a pencil or pen but then I became rather good at using the computer.

There have been times when I've looked at what was written and wonder where it came from. Then there is some stuff that just blows my mind. I've written letters, poems and have even drawn a couple of pictures in my day. I have received messages for other people and that sometimes is a tricky thing. I just can't go up to someone and tell them I received this mes-sage for them from the spirit world. That's a one way trip to the mental hos-pital. I have given poems to people only because I know they can handle it, that they are open to the idea of the spirit world and things of that nature. So those are easy. It's hard when the message you receive is meant for someone who might not be so open to such communication.

Some spirits have been known to bug me until I write the message down and pass it off. That happened to me for one of my co-workers. A real close friend of his died, a girl I didn't know at all and to be honest I didn't know my co-worker that well either. I also knew that he was religious, and for some a message from your dead friend isn't exactly welcomed with open arms. So I did the only thing I could do. I typed up the message, which actually was a poem, and left it in his mailbox. He didn't know who left it or where it came from until he left the company, as I gave him the poem again in a frame with a picture of a long winding road surrounded by trees.

I wrote a letter to explain how the poem came to be and I was pleasantly surprised that he was so accepting of it. So much so, that he said it was the best good-bye gift he'd gotten. Most of the time, I do the anonymous thing because you just never know how a person will react. Same thing goes for channeling. I would only channel in front of a newbie if they were okay with me doing it. I always felt that the people you're with should be comfortable before you do something because having someone scared and frightened is not a good thing. You want them to have a good experience.

Good experiences are important when using a Ouija board, channeling and doing pretty much anything else. If a session is good, chances are what people feared going into it will slowly go away. Plus, they're likely to join you the next time you do it. Kind of like food: if you like the taste of chocolate, chances are you will eat it again. By no means is a Ouija board a toy. It's a serious mediumistic tool and not just a game. Most people have bad connotations about Ouija boards saying they're evil and all this other mumbo jumbo. For me, I take the Ouija board very seriously. If used with good intentions, any session you have with it will be good as well. If you're looking to have fun and get scared then that will happen to you.

The Ouija board stuff kicked into gear in the second half of the first semester. At this point, Michael had helped me out and I was transforming. I was waking up to life after being dead to it for so long. Kind of ironic if you think about it; I'm communicating with the dead in order to feel alive.

My transformation from the depressive-suicidal to the happy person was not easy and it didn't happen overnight. I constantly fought it in the beginning, slipping now and then, but not slipping to the point where I'd start having thoughts of killing myself. No, slipping for me was just getting really depressed and crying a lot.

Art became my out for the pain still lurking in me. I would draw what was creeping around inside of me. The thoughts with the intent to kill myself have been dormant for fifteen years now. My life is not perfect. I readily admit that I get depressed for a few days or for a few months out of the year, especially during the fall.

Michael and I were closer than ever that semester and one night we got together with my Ouija board. By this time, it had been used a lot by

Raine and me. It had its own vibe. I took very good care of my board and I wouldn't let anyone use it unless I was there. (I broke this rule later on). You could pick up the planchette and feel this strong pull coming from the board, it was that cool. At first, I thought it was just me that could feel this pull. Michael felt it too, although I told him about the sensation. However, there were a few others I didn't tell who commented that it felt like the planchette was being pulled to the board.

One night, on the third floor of Standard dorm in room 321, eleven people gathered for a night of fun which turned into an emotional rollercoaster for some. It was a night that some friendships ended, never to be repaired from the damage that took place. It was also a night that those of us with unique gifts were shunned. The spring semester wasn't even a month old.

I can't recall who was there exactly but I think I can make a good guess: Michael, Jake, Sarah Jones, Heidi Waters, Anna Wilcox, Donna Waites, Olga Ozarkowski, Willa Crowley, Melanie Kerr, Janet Nichols, and one girl whose name I can't flipping remember.

We huddled into Sarah and Janet's tiny dorm room. Michael was using the board with Jake who lived on the fourth floor. At first the usual remarks of "You're pushing it," were being accused all over the place, but that wasn't the case. Jake spoke up right away to say that neither he nor Michael was pushing the planchette. I sat behind Michael and unknown to the rest of the room I knew we had a visitor. Michael did too, and would look over his shoulder to flash me a look. The neat trick they all freaked about and then thought was cool was the cold spot on Michael's left. There was a distinct temperature change. It was always more fun when Michael's left arm was cold and his right warm. Michael's left arm was normally warm but during this night of adventure his left arm was cold for a little while. I should note that Michael had a slightly cruel sense of humor and as it turned out, so did Shadow, and well....me too.

The whole point of the night was to have fun, but no, someone had to go and ruin it. Just for the record I was not the first one to ruin it. Janet asked if Shadow could do something to prove that he was real. He said sure and then this big crash happened outside the door to the room. Everyone got up to go look and a framed picture that had been on the wall was now on the floor in pieces.

So everyone had a minor freak-out except for Michael and me. It seemed so natural to us and watching everyone else react was funny. Then the next stage of ruining the night began as Lewis Whitehall and Eric Chance joined in on the fun. Lewis was out to prove that Michael was playing tricks and stuff. Lewis wasn't very fond of Michael for whatever reason. He decided to ask for details regarding the death of his friend. Shadow refused.

I told Lewis, as did Michael, that you don't ask about dead friends or ask about dates. I can't remember the reason why, it was just something you didn't do. Lewis however wanted to know; he wanted details and Shadow wasn't willing to tell him.

I think Lewis argued for a good ten minutes and then I could feel the tension in the room. I could sense that Shadow was going to fix Lewis real good. Lewis wanted information so Shadow decided he was going to lie about everything. Of course, Lewis took the opportunity to call Michael a fraud, joke that the Ouija board was fake and well, you get the picture. I took great offense to that and then someone else wanted to know about a dead friend.

Willa had a friend who committed suicide and Shadow said once again he was not going to reveal information and even Michael and I told her no way. You don't ask about such things, but Willa wanted to know if her friend was okay which Shadow was willing to tell her: yes. Shadow did not want to tell Willa anything else. I just couldn't take it anymore and I blurted it all out. How he died, the location and what he was wearing. I had the information in my head. It was coming in pictures and I was picking it up from Shadow and Michael knew that I had. Once I blurted everything out, that was the end of the party. Willa was shaking and upset. She lived next door, climbed into bed and put on a Disney movie. Others went to their rooms but it was so late that most everyone stayed in Sarah and Janet's room – the whole safety in numbers thing. That's when my vision of an iron gate came real strong and I could see a cloaked figure inviting me to come closer. I wasn't sure what to make of it. It freaked everyone out since the figure was in front of a cemetery. They assumed it invoked the feeling of suicide in me although I didn't want to kill myself. Once everyone calmed down and convinced that I was okay, we went to bed. I remember waking up in the middle of the night to find Michael standing over me. The moonlight shone through the window highlighting half of his face. It's like I woke up knowing he'd be there.

Two or three hours later, zombie like, I managed to make it to breakfast with Michael, Anna and Donna who were still freaked out from seeing a Shadow in their bathroom. Breakfast proved to be interesting because there was this girl, Elaine Dwyer, who always visited my suite and would yell for one of my suitemates on the days I had late morning classes. Nothing pisses you off more if your class isn't until eleven a.m. and someone screams and wakes you up at eight a.m. At breakfast I spotted her and thought "bitch" and next thing I know Michael sits down next to me and says "Who's a bitch?" I was totally taken aback. How did he know what I was thinking?

From that day on, Michael and I grew closer and my friends from the night before drifted apart. They were so scared that all of them except Anna and Donna went to the school counselor and had a session. In this session, they suggested that I be committed to a mental institution due to (1) the stuff I said to Willa and (2) because of my vision of the gate.

This is where things get interesting. Because of this meeting about me, Michael's name also popped up. Next thing I know I'm getting a phone call from the school counselor telling me to stay away from Michael, his Head Resident is telling him to stay away from me and my Head Resident is also notified of what's going on. I actually got told that if there were any more "paranormal" things going on in the dorm I could be booted off campus. What crap.

Needless to say, this brought Michael and me together even more. If they thought we were hanging out too much before, well, we showed them what hanging out really was. I think they all just realized they should give up and stop trying to keep us apart. Seriously, like the college has the right to tell me who I can or cannot be friends with.

I was so mad at my friends that they quickly became ex-friends for even suggesting I be put in a mental hospital. I didn't talk to any of them for about two to three months. They definitely pissed me off.

Journal Excerpt:
CSC Senior Year (1ˢᵗ Year)
February 8, 1993

> *I hate my friends, I hate my friends.*
> *I hate my back-stabbing, two faced friends,*
> *And now since the attitude is shown*
> *I think I'll take a gun so they'll get blown.*
> *I used to enjoy the times we shared*
> *But now I know better for I've had my share.*
> *Now it's my turn to play the game,*
> *To make their lives totally insane.*

Like I said, that whole night, the following day and what the school did really pissed me off. That poem was just the start of a rant.

Journal Excerpt:
CSC Senior Year (1ˢᵗ Year)
February 8, 1993

STOP! Whoa Maynard – calm down! I don't think they're your friends anymore. NO THEY'RE NOT! TWO TIMING TRAITORS. OK – so they're not the greatest people in the world. THEY HAVE NOTHING BETTER TO DO THAN RAG ON MY OTHER FRIENDS – I'M JUST PLAIN GETTING TIRED OF IT.

> *Journal Excerpt:*
> *February 8, 1993 (continued)*
>
> *Telling them off is not the key. You've been doing a good job of ignoring them because you know you don't need them. You're a senior and they're sophomores, they have yet to grow up. Clear your mind, it's 11:05, think of better things to think about than these losers – make class fun, not a living hell. Don't waste your time and energy on these low lifes. You don't need them. Your true friends will be back next semester. Keira, Raine and Michael are your true friends. They understand you.*

I told you I was ticked off. I should note that at the time this journal entry was written, Michael had broken his leg while skiing and suffered a double fracture, Raine had problems at home and Keira needed a break. All three of them left CSC to come back the following fall semester. What a lonely spring semester it was for me. No more Ouija board with them and me off on my own to find myself; my identity.

Amazingly, word had gotten around campus about my Ouija board and other paranormal skills. This caused a few people to be scared of me. Plus, my long internalized anger was now surfacing and I was getting in people's faces a bit.

Basically, I was just tired of being walked all over like a mat. I was starting to find my voice, to come alive. Yet through all of this, I was still the invisible girl in some ways and I often wondered if anybody was listening to me.

CHAPTER TEN

"Don't Give Up On Me, I'm About To Come Alive" - Train

Journal Excerpt:
CSC Senior Year (1st Year)
February 22, 1993

   "I'm not addicted to the board. I find it fun and interesting. It has opened my eyes to a few things. On 2/10 you [my English Professor] asked us to write about truth – my way of thinking about truth came from my experiences on the board and a book called "Messages from Michael" by Chelsea Yarbo. I guess I have a better understanding of things. I've found belief. You know that some people ask themselves "Who am I?" and say they "have to go find themselves," I think I'm finding myself out right now, finding out who I am. Things have fallen into place as far as my life goes. I'm very calm now about things, I'm more relaxed and mature. I've done a lot of growing up but the majority of that growing up has come this semester.

   For six years I have lived with depression and suicide. Maynard Clark the loner. For the past three years life has been hell, and I've been at high risk. I come to college to start over and improve myself and instead I get worse. I've seen Sue Ellen Kennedy for the better part of two years here at Caledonia. She has helped me out only because I wanted to get out of what I was living. You can't get better unless you're willing to help yourself.

   This semester Sue Ellen has said that I look better – not so tense and my attitude about things is very mature. Chloe Fuller my advisor is pleased so far with my academics this semester – Maynard Clark got her butt in gear! Yes, Maynard Clark got her butt in gear, actually Maynard Clark got her life together.

Journal Excerpt:
February 22, 1993 (continued)

It took sometime, a lot of pain, confusion and uncertainty has come in the last six years but this year things have come together. About December of '92 is when everything was falling into place. Whether or not me using the Ouija board had anything to do with my change I'm not sure but I think it did affect me a little. Actually, I think the book helped more. Things were put into a different perspective.

It must sound weird to you and it sounds weird to me. But looking back on last semester, there was one person who saved me. Around October, (I think Oct. 14th but I'm not sure) I snapped, reaching out for help and no one was reaching back until I ran into Michael. For the first time <u>*EVER*</u>*, I actually said what I needed, what I wanted and what I was feeling. Michael was there for me. I spoke my mind, he listened. I was scared and unstable. Before I found him, I had visited the library roof but denied the ground below. Michael stayed with me a long time and then I listened to him for awhile.*

After that night he was everything to me. Friendship was not friendship anymore."

With Michael's help and the Ouija board, I was coming alive. I was changing. I was opening up, learning more about myself and trying to understand the things that happened to me. I was still dealing with old patterns, trying hard to break free from that endless tape loop of negativity that played in my brain. I was breaking free, I was coming alive and for the first time in a long time, I felt fine.

I still had a lot of work to do, but as my journal entry suggests I was doing rather well at the time. My friends may have left me and old friends were not worth my time but it left me with some other friends that I didn't get the chance to really appreciate. One of those friends was Keith Campbell.

What can be said about Keith besides the fact that he's a great guy? Keith was good for me, he was older and wiser than Michael. If I were to draw a family tree, Keith would be the oldest brother, Michael would be the middle child and I would be the baby sister. In college, your friends are your family in some aspects. Keith also had the best hugs. In order to explain how important he was to me, I will share this unsent letter with all of you. I never sent it to him and as I write this I think that I should, to let him know that he made a difference.

Journal Excerpt:
February 22, 2006

Dear Keith,

     I started to write in my journal on the bus that I hardly ever write about you which is surprising considering how much you meant to me. I spend a lot of time writing about Michael and other people but for some reason I don't write a lot about you. So today, I'm writing about you and only you. I may mention others because I have to in relation to you but this is your time in the spotlight.

     You meant as much to me as Michael did. You were the big brother, you were older than I, you had more life experience and it was that wisdom I tapped into now and then, getting your advice about stuff. It was nice to have such a friend as you to confide in and trust. When I hugged you, I felt warm on the inside and knew in that moment that you would never let anything bad happen to me. In a way, you were my Merlin, my Obi-Wan Kenobi with your wise words and insights.

     It was the moments alone that I loved the most with you. I also felt smart talking with you, that we were on some higher level that the others couldn't grasp. I remember your hugs, I remember sitting at the Miss Caledonia Diner having a hot chocolate with you when I was near penniless on a rainy night in the dead of winter.

     Michael helped me emotionally but you helped me intellectually. You were always a smart cookie and so talented in graphic design and English. You were the only mature and confident friend I had but you knew how to have fun. You were the type of guy a girl would marry because you were in many ways Prince Charming. You were supportive, caring, listened well and had a twinkle in your eyes that showed your love of life. You were safe and it was okay for me to be me around you. You came into my life when I needed someone to help balance out what Michael was helping me with. Michael was helping my emotional side while you were helping me out mentally. Whatever I felt for Michael, I felt it for you too, this I just now realize. If I was stranded on an island it would be you and Michael I would want to have with me. You deserve some credit too for helping to create who I am today. It scares me to think where I would be if I had I not met you when I did.

     My only regret is that I never told you how important you were to me back then. Perhaps it's because I didn't realize it until just now.

Journal Excerpt:
February 22, 2006 (continued)

You are the original Keith and since you, guys named Keith have come into my life when I am at my lowest and the strangest thing is they all resemble you in appearance. It's quite interesting to see it happen but I welcome it gladly. The most recent Keith, I have never spoken to but he appeared at a low point in my life and a year after seeing him for the first time he still makes me happy. When I have a bad day I sometimes go to his place of work and look for him. The sight of him makes me feel better and while he is a reflection of my inner me, there is a part of me that acknowledges you too. I carry you around with me all the time but you are buried in me, you are a silent part of me that is always there. You are warmth, strength, comfort and safety. No harm will ever come when I am with you. Perhaps this is why these various Keith's pop up in my life to not only remind me to keep going and have hope that things will get better but to know that I am always safe because I carry a part of you with me - always.

You are my Methos [A character from Highlander TV series]. Wise and compassionate. You are the survivor, you have triumphed in your life and those things were given to me by you. Michael gave me my sword but you showed me how to use it. You showed me that I could be that strong and if I ever faltered not to worry because all I had to do was look or think of you. You are my Merlin, my Obi-Wan Kenobi, my Methos, my Prince, my Angel.....my Keith. Thank you. Thank you for being so much more than just a friend to me.

Love always - Maynard

Ah, Keith, so much the brother. He was always the perfect gentleman and had such a beautiful inner light. That dolphin ring he gave us is a cherished gift, safely kept in a box and only worn once in a while to help calm our nerves, to give us strength when we face uncertainty like the time we went in for diagnosis of our medical condition.

We wore that ring that day and things didn't seem so bad. We wore that ring to a couple of job interviews, too.

Every time Mariah Carey's "Anytime You Need A Friend" comes on the radio we think of him. That was our song with him and to this day it brings back such good memories.

Keith is the type of guy we need with a bit of the mischievous and good side of Michael. Of all the guys that have come into your life, they made the most impact even though you didn't know it at the time. Only now do you finally get it; only now do you appreciate such a wondrous gift. When we wish someone would hold us, it's Keith or Michael we think of because they are the only ones who ever made us feel wanted and safe. They are the only ones we've really ever opened up to with no fear of being rejected.

CHAPTER ELEVEN

"I Want To Know What Love Is" - Foreigner

It is a pattern that has followed me for a long time, this need to be wanted and to have worth. For so much of my life I have been rejected and when I am accepted it's hard because I wait for something bad to happen. I wait to be stabbed in the back. Trust is an issue because I have so often been betrayed by people who say they are my friends.

In my entire life I've had all of three boyfriends. One lasted three weeks and the other two lasted six months a piece. I haven't had a boyfriend since 1998 and to be honest I've grown accustomed to being alone. I don't like being alone and lonely all the time but I'm used to it. Sure, part of me is a bit jealous of those around me with their boyfriends and what not and I wonder what's wrong with me. Then again I'm not out and about town hitting bars and such. Bars and I are not a good idea. I don't dare drink anymore in the off chance I may trigger something.

Friends may say I'm extroverted but believe me I've very introverted. I'm shy and quiet and often the observer in a room full of people. Some habits are hard to break and to be honest I've never had the social skills to really interact with people. I get by pretty well but sometimes I just want to kick myself. Over the years and even recently I interact with guys that are nice and we seem to have stuff in common, but I always get stuck with the asking out part. I just never seem to do it. Even when I used to do it in college, it was nothing but rejection after rejection. Maybe part of me has just given up. The thing is I'm not really looking for a boyfriend anymore. It's not what I want, or maybe it is, I don't know. What I really want most of all is to be held. To feel a guy wrap his arms around me, his hand in my hair with his head to mine and just let me cry. I know, it probably doesn't make sense but it's true. I say that I want to cry and that's because *Inner Me* needs it, I need that. To feel a guy hold me and tell me everything will be fine. Then again a nice hug would do me some good. I haven't been hugged by a guy that makes me feel the way Michael and Keith would make me feel. I miss that feeling of inner warmth. I experience it now and then with one of my male co-workers, but as much as I would like to linger in a hug with him I simply can't because he is a co-worker. It's probably not a good idea on my part to hug him for a long time even though I want to lest anyone gets the wrong idea.

What I really want is to hang out with a guy I guess. Someone I can curl up with on a couch and watch a movie with. Someone I can sit on a park bench with and watch people. Someone I can sit in a café or restaurant and enjoy a peaceful time with. Someone I can be in a room with but be doing my own thing while they do their own thing. It's just nice to be in a room with someone else even if you aren't interacting with each other. I suppose I just want someone to enjoy the journey with.

That sounds good to me. A guy I can confide in who will accept me for who I am along with all my faults. The company of a guy sounds so simple but has been hard to find. Maybe it's because I haven't been looking that hard and for me, guys are troubled waters.

A lack of a boyfriend was one of the contributing factors to my super slide into depression and suicide. For the longest time I believed all the things others told me, that I was indeed an ugly reject and no guy would go out with me. Perhaps this is why I mourn for Michael so much sometimes because he was my friend, but he was more than that. He was this middle ground between friend and boyfriend. Keith was sort of there too but it was mostly with Michael. I was able to be close to Michael without getting rejected. If I needed a hug, no problem, I just had to ask.

I have this fantasy of coming home from work, laying down in bed and some guy, any guy, pulling me close to him as I take a nap for an hour. No words exchanged between us, just him holding me as I let myself go, let myself just completely relax and make myself vulnerable I guess, knowing that I'm safe in the arms of the guy I'm with. All of us have so many walls around ourselves that we often never ever let down our guards and to be honest, I really just want to let all of mine down. With Michael I could sort of do that and to an extent I could do it with Keith, too. I never curled up with either one of them because that would have been just wrong at the time since they both had girlfriends, but their hugs filled that feeling.

It's nice knowing that you're wanted. It's nice to receive a hug and know that it's genuine and that the person you are receiving it from really does care about you. You know it when you get one because something inside you tells you its okay to let it all out. Well, that's how it is for me. So often we hug people but it's not genuine and I admit that I'd probably break down and cry from a genuine hug since I haven't had one in ages. It's the kind of hug that lets you know you matter to someone.

This is something that has plagued me for a long time – do I matter? So often I think I don't. I know it's the old part of me that has that train of thought. It's been hard after all the years to convince myself that I do matter. I see all my friends in relationships and wonder will I ever feel the one thing they all have – love. I want to know what love is because I've never had it. I've only brushed by love.

What about my parents, right? HA! Please. Doesn't matter how many damn birthday cards signed "Love, Mom and Dad" I get, they are just words. They're empty words. To be honest, those words, the magic words of "I love you" have never been uttered to me by them. I come from what I call an unemotional family. The last time I think I was ever hugged by my dad was age six. I can't even remember the last time my mom hugged me. Here's a quick synopsis of my childhood: dinner time consisted of us being in the same room but not sitting together at a table, as time went on we eventually stopped eating in the same room. We all went to separate rooms. The only time we are in the same room for meals these days is for Thanksgiving and Christmas. For the most part my parents left me alone to play in my room as there were no kids my age in my neighborhood. The only thing my parents made me do that I didn't want to besides yard work was going to Catechism classes and going to Easter Mass.

I hated going to church because well, I just hated going. See, my dad is Catholic and I was raised Catholic but my mom is Protestant. My family was basically like Ireland. The Catholics and Protestants were always butting heads. My parents had no idea I was depressed and suicidal because I was such a good girl. I never caused any trouble, I was just quiet.

I have no true concept of love. Sure, I can open a dictionary and get a definition but I don't know what love really is. It wasn't until after I under-stood my friendship with Michael that I grasped the concept of unconditional love. It took me thirteen years to figure that out!

Maybe the reason I can't grasp the concept of love is because well, unlike those my age, I haven't been completely intimate with another. I've fooled around with guys but there is one thing I haven't done. I used to be ashamed of being pure as snow because society puts this evil spin on it. I'm just a bit old fashioned I guess.

Perhaps it's my Catholic upbringing talking but you don't have sex until you are married. I don't ever plan on getting married because I see it as a hassle. Besides, the majority of people I went to high school and college with are all getting divorces, so why should I put myself through that kind of hell? Plus, I have my parents to thank for this outlook on marriage.

All through my high school years all my parents ever did was yell at each other which caused me to wonder when they would break up. Needless to say, they're still together. I have an old fashioned view that if I'm going to get married than that night I should lose my virginity and therefore I'm loved. That's a fucked up idea, isn't it? There's a part of me that just once wishes to do the deed but yet there is another part of me that wants to adhere to the no sex before marriage thing. Then there's a part of me who says "who gives a shit, do what you want." So I guess I fall under the "it will either happen or it won't" category.

It's a catch twenty-two because I really need to experience touch by another person. Like I said, being held and hugged or laying down next to a guy is a big deal for me. The little girl that lurks inside me is desperate for touch, desperate to feel what love is and I'm not one hundred percent sure how to get this for us. It's like the Foreigner song. I wish someone could show me what love is because it is a concept that I cannot completely grasp. I'm not so much interested in the sex part of love because you can love someone without being intimate with them. I guess it's more of the emotional part and as I mentioned before just being held. I want to feel the love that comes with doing those things. Maybe the love I have for Michael is the closest I'll ever know of what love can be. I really don't know.

You are so pathetic. Can you believe the shit that's spewing from her? Haven't had a boyfriend in a zillion years, have never had sex. Boo Hoo. Get a Kleenex box. You fat ugly cow, you'll never get a guy looking the way you do. What guy in his right mind would want to hang out with you? What guy would want to hug you? Besides you're not the right kind of girl for guys to hug up to because you don't dress like a girl should. Doesn't matter how fucking nice you are, sweetheart, you'll never get a guy because society says you have to be skinny and real women wear make-up, which you don't and believe me you should. Have you seen yourself in the mirror lately? Plus, you do nothing but jeans and shirts, when you're home its t-shirts and sweat pants. Oh La La...you're so attractive. A real regular guy magnet.

Will you shut the fuck up? What you see is what you get and if you don't like what you're looking at, look elsewhere! Wearing make-up makes us feel like we aren't being authentic to the world. Besides, why should we change who we are to impress some guy? If a guy can't see that there's more to us then it's his loss.

You're scared little girl, aren't you? Why don't you go hide under a rock.

Yes, I admit it, I'm scared to get close to someone only because the times I have gotten really close to people I always end up getting hurt, really hurt. The times where I have told someone something, fully opened myself up to them I have always gotten hurt.

They've used what I said against me or blabbed it all over the place. So yes, I have trust issues, too. I don't trust people for the most part. I test everybody. I may share something with them and see what they do or don't do with it. I then make the decision if I can trust them or not. I know it sounds a bit mean. Considering how much people have hurt me over the years, I'm just protecting myself.

Sure, there may be one or two who pass my test and then turn out to be people I should have never have trusted. Then again, there is the test but I listen to my gut, too. I listen to *Inner Me*. If I get the creeps from you, it'll be awhile before I tell you anything. Hell, I currently have a medical condition and I've told all of five people what I actually have. I've been living with it for about two years, and my parents don't even know. Most surprisingly, the one friend who I've known for sixteen years doesn't even know. Want to know why I haven't told my friend? Because I know they won't be emotionally supportive for me.

I have few friends, but of the few I have, they don't all know the same thing. One friend may know one thing but that doesn't mean another friend will know it. It's called selective sharing I guess. Makes sense to me. If I'm going to get burned, it's best to be burned by only one friend instead of all of them at once. These are my defense mechanisms. When you have lived the life I have, you kind of need them.

Getting close to people is scary, as I've never ever really let anyone get too close. Sure, I slept with two of my three boyfriends. When I say slept, I mean actually sleep. I've also been in a couple of situations where I was almost sexually assaulted by overly anxious guys. Luckily, I acted quickly, but talk about scary. Back then, the feel of a warm body next to me was good enough for me because for once I wasn't so scared. I felt safe. I know, safe from what? To be honest, I think I have been so insecure for such a long time that I need someone else to make me feel secure because I can't always do it myself. I'm still working on this but I'm not sure how to do it. I just do the best I can. I need others to be my Stuart Smalley. You know, the character from Saturday Night Live whose daily affirmation was - *"I'm smart enough, I'm good enough, and gosh darn it, people like me!"*

For so long people hated me and picked on me, so it's nice to have people genuinely like me. Yes, I know I shouldn't need to do things to make people like me. People will like me or they won't but acceptance has been something else that I have missed in my life. It's important that people somewhat like me I suppose. I don't want to be the person people cringe about although I'm sure there are some people who do when my name is mentioned.

It shouldn't matter what others think of me but all those years of depression were founded on what other people thought of me. I said it once, I'll say it again, it's very hard to break the cycle and even I fall into my old pat-

terns sometimes because I know them so well. It's almost comforting sometimes to slip back but I know that I can never linger there for too long. I don't
ever want to become the person I once was.

I don't ever want to waste my life to suicidal thoughts and depression. I can't be those things again. I acknowledge that it will always be a part
of me but I will not let it rule me. I will not let it take the driver seat of my
proverbial car. I'm driving it now, *Inner Me* is hunkered down in the passen-
ger seat and the **Saboteur** is in the backseat, with Suicide & Depression sitting in the car seat. That's the way this car has to drive and if ever the **Saboteur** or Suicide & Depression claim the driver seat again, I'm screwed.

Journal Excerpt:
January 31, 2006

*I'm a fragile little girl who at any moment could break and
that's not good. The little girl can handle being broke but not for long
because the decision then has to be made to put her together again or
just sweep her up and dump her in the trash. No one loves the little girl
and hasn't for a long time but at this point, a hug or some sort of affection would be nice for her. She wants to feel needed not rejected.*

*I wish the damn little girl would shut up!! I hear you little girl
but I don't know how to fix us. If we were depressed and suicidal then
I'd know how to fix us but this, I don't know what to do. I know what
you need so we can co-exist but I don't know how to get what you need.
I see people who might be able to help but I don't have the skills to ask
for what I want or what you want. I never have and you know that. I
am rebuilding and restructuring to give us a better foundation. We
have been fragmented for years and I've patched us together as best as
possible. We survived a lot of pain and I know it's still there, it always
will be but give me credit for getting us this far. I am exhausted and
tired of holding us together but I do it because neither you nor I deserve to be where we once were. I'll find the affection that you so desperately crave. I promise but give me more time. You can't rebuild and
rediscover yourself overnight, it takes time and I'm sure once I give us
a much stronger foundation that everything else will fall into place. If I
can't rebuild us on my own then I'll try to find someone who can help
us.*

*Michael's not here to help us and neither is Keith. We're on
our own this time. It's scary I know but we'll make it. We have to. We
have no other choice but to keep going.*

It took me seven years to get into the driver seat. If all that pain ever reclaims that spot, will I have the strength to take control again? It's something I can't answer and actually fear. That's why I try my best to stay where I'm at. I don't want to live in gloom and doom and if I do, how long will it grip me and will it ever let me go again? Will I be able to break free in a week, a month, a year? I feel depression's tentacles reaching out to me all the time but I move forward and work to make sure it can't wrap me up again. I have been suicide free for fifteen years and I'd like to keep adding years to that. I do get bummed out and depressed sometimes but it's not as dark as those seven years of hell. I have come a long way to be where I'm at and I'm scared as hell that I may never have this life again if suicide grips me.

I don't have Michael or Keith to help me. All the major players who helped me the first time around are gone. All there is… is me. Oops, almost forgot Def Leppard…Steve Clark and a whole slew of people I don't even know. Still, I can't easily access them like I could Michael or Keith.

It's nice having these reminders, these mechanisms to stay strong, to have faith but if there is no person for me to physically touch then I'm in trouble. It's that comfort from another, it's their heartbeat that reminds me I am alive and I have to fight to stay alive. My self worth is once more on display in someone else, reflecting back to me that I do have something to offer this world even if sometimes I don't think I do.

CHAPTER TWELVE

"From The Inside" – Def Leppard

Is it my turn? Yes! Finally I can talk.

I am the Saboteur, the critic if you will, or in some cases Miss Negativity. Whatever, they all apply to me. I am the destroyer. I am the voice that reinforces stupidity, worthlessness, insecurity, loneliness. I am the voice that helps drive a person toward depression and then to suicide. Boy did I drive the car good. All the material I needed to send her spinning into Hell was provided by cruel, snobby rich kids who thought they ruled the world. Her parents didn't pay attention to her which helped out even more. What a poor only child. All she had were her imaginary friends to play with. Friends were near zero for her because quite honestly she was a zero and even now after she's "claimed" she's better she still hardly has any friends. I may be sitting in the back seat of the proverbial car she's driving, but believe me folks I'm within stabbing range since I'm sitting right behind her. I know exactly what to do to gain control of the car.

You're probably wondering why I don't go for it again. Well, to be honest, the kid deserves a break. Believe me though, I'm not silent. I still fire off a few insults now and then. I torture her still because it's fun. I plant the seed of doubt in her and mess her up sometimes so that she ends up destroying something good. What can I say? When it comes to guys I pride myself on knowing I have ruined it for her on more than one occasion.

Don't feel too bad for her folks. I am the darkness that walks with her every day. I am the one that reaches out from the fog to wrap her up in my vicious tentacles, calling to her to join me once more. She can't get rid of me. I am always here, just not as loud as I once was. I miss the old days when I ruled her a bit more. I miss filling her head with all those bad thoughts. My personal favorite lines that I used on her all the time were:

1) No one wants you, go ahead, kill yourself
2) You're ugly, you're worthless, you're pathetic
3) No one will miss you if you're dead
4) Your life sucks, just do it. Kill yourself, end the pain.
5) There's no reason to live, no will miss you if you die. Go ahead. Die!

I miss saying those to her but even just saying them now they've lost a bit of their edge, their bite. She still feels me, folks, as I sit back here in the car and kick her seat like the pain in the ass I am. I love my job. I suppose in some ways you might think I was trying to save her by telling her to kill herself. All this doom and gloom, this tormented life she was leading - what better way to end the pain but for her to die? Just die...die...die.

I helped her run away from home when she was in the fifth grade. Of course, our young mind hadn't quite figured out the logistics and we ended up running away to school after hours. She was to meet up with another classmate but it just didn't happen that way. It was a pitiful running away because three hours later she went home and mommy and daddy didn't even notice. They thought she was out playing in the backyard. No sit down talk about it at all. Totally fucking ignored the whole situation. What a way to reinforce that she's not worthy. Parents are so fucking stupid, not just hers. Kids fire off warning signs all the time and yet get ignored time and time again. I love it and yet hate it at the same time. There's nothing more pitiful than clueless parents who blindly go through life thinking their kids are okay and for the most part their kids probably are but geez...get a clue and pay attention.

What drove her to run away, I don't remember. She was young and stupid. However, it marked the beginning of the depression, it would come but it wasn't until high school that it kicked in hard. She was in elementary school and the depression train was put on the track. It moved slowly until she hit high school and like a bullet from a gun, the train ran with a fury.

In high school she was isolated. She may have been there but she was invisible to all around her. Her clothes isolated her, her lack of being in a clique isolated her, the type of music she listened to isolated her, everything about who she was isolated her. She was the outsider always looking in, trying to find a group to belong to but she wasn't worthy at all. She wasn't worthy of anyone's time. Even some of her teachers ignored her. As much as she tried to fit in she was always the outcast and when she signed up for the vocational program her junior year that too isolated her. For two years she spent half of her days at another school to learn technical electronics in a classroom with twenty-two guys and a teacher who was a chauvinist.

Through her odd nature she amazingly almost fit in with them. The guys picked on her but she was gaining respect, a bit of worth. She was so fragile that those good things didn't last for long because I took them away. I spread in her head a venomous anti-worth toxin that simply destroyed her piece by piece until she couldn't handle the world she was living in. The pain was strong and I just pushed her as much as I could, let the thoughts become reality, let the thoughts of death creep into her mind and into her dreams. There in her dreams I insulted her too. So many times she killed herself in her dreams, as if killing herself would somehow make all the pain go away and that a new version of her would come alive. Foolish child.

College was a blast because alcohol came into her world. Boy, what a lethal toxin that was fueled with a few Tylenol just for fun. Even drunk out of her mind I worked my magic bringing her down into the depths of a dark wasteland, a dark forest of serpentine thoughts. There really was no reason for her to live, not a single one. Even a few months into college the rejection came, harsher than it had been in high school. College was the ultimate reinforcement of her insecurities, her worthlessness and in a sea of college students she would be missed once again.

She basically was just her social security number to the college and might as well have been to her roommate, suitemates and anyone else she encountered.

No matter how many flags she flew up no one paid attention until it was almost too late. When help finally did arrive, what did the fucking school want to do but take that help away. HA HA HA HA!

I drove her as best I could to death but the one thing I didn't count on was her embracing it so much. She found comfort in death. She did not fear it even when she looked Death right in the eyes. No shit, she managed to actually meet Death. Very few meet Death and live to tell about it but she did and she happily embraced the spiritual tour guide that he was. She found comfort in Death. She found comfort in the swampland, in the dark forest. She was walking in the valley of the shadow of death and she feared no evil. Damn girl ruined all my fun but then again, Michael was the one who really ruined my fun – bastard.

The harder I tried to end her life, to put the pain to bed, the more she tried to live, the more that weak little part of her grew in strength. The battle had been going for years and I was kicking ass but then Michael came along, then Keith and that weak little part of her started to grow stronger and suddenly I found myself sitting in the damn backseat of this stinking car! I'm in this car but I'm not happy and one day, one day she'll slip and I'll drive the car again. You hear me girly, I'm going to drive this car again someday and when I do the seven years of hell you went through will be nothing compared to the new reign of terror I will bring. I know you fear me taking control, I sense weakness and this time Def Leppard records aren't going to save your ass.

CHAPTER THIRTEEN

"To Be Alive" - Clock

    *Well, now that the **Saboteur** has spoken I guess I get my chance although I have spoken plenty so far. It is true the **Saboteur** did her best to kill us all but the **Saboteur** is smart in the fact that dying would have meant the end to her as well. It is hard to explain to anyone the why's and how's of wanting to kill oneself. After all these years, I don't think there is a clear cut reason or one incident that triggered this all to happen. It was a culmination of a lot of events and vocalized abuse.*

    When you don't get what you need from those around you, it's hard to find it on your own. How easy is it for an eight year old to not internalize hateful words from another person? It's not easy at all. It's not easy to take all that negativity and keep it externalized. Eventually all those hateful words become internalized and when they do it's hard not to turn them into something even more sinister.

    I don't know if I can present the picture in a way for you, the reader, to understand. It's hard to tell someone what it's like to be suicidal if they have never experienced feelings of deep sorrow, of desperation, of feeling trapped and pushed into a corner. The total sum of your problems are consuming you and pushing you into a corner and all you can do to get out is possibly end your life. All of us have this trap door but only a few ever touch the door knob or even open the door. The pain one feels when standing at Death's door is unlike any pain ever felt or imagined. It is everything coming at you at once. Everything is magnified ten fold in the mind of a depressed, suicidal prisoner. I say prisoner because that's what life becomes: a prison. You're trapped within the confines of your mind, and the messages are non-stop as they urge you to kill yourself. You are trapped by your own thoughts and all you desperately want to do is to escape from them.

    As I mentioned before I am the crying girl that resides inside. I am sixteen, although part of me is very much like a little girl about eight years old. It doesn't really matter how old I am, the fact remains I am a crying girl and I am still fragile to an extent. I have done the best to help us survive under the conditions we grew up with. Children just do not have the resources to deal with such intense emotions. Their coping mechanisms have not been built yet. I did what I could with what I had and what the world gave to us. I tried many things to help her but it was music, the last resort to saving her, which saved us.

*I tried steering her toward the people I thought could help but they all turned a blind eye to us. I tried using her talent of writing to get help but got another blind look from those that read her scriptures. Frustration, anger and sadness ran rampant through me. The meadow that's so beautiful now was a disaster zone back then. Weeds were everywhere in the meadow and I hated the little house. Even the oak tree looked decrepit. Everything was falling apart and I didn't have the glue to keep it all together I was desperate and in a losing battle with the **Saboteur** but I wasn't willing to give up.*

I had to fight for us. I had to find something to keep us going. Music was the last idea I had and if it didn't work, that would be the end of us.

Backed into the corner, with the door open to Death, I was hoping, scratching, and in panic mode trying to keep us alive.

*Every attempt she made to end her life I was in combat with the **Saboteur** but with each attempt the **Saboteur** seemed to add more fuel to the fire. The **Saboteur** used the opportunity to beat her down some more, telling her that she was a failure. Every failed attempt to take her life she felt even more worthless, increasing the need to end her life. The **Saboteur** was in some ways so focused on getting her to kill herself that I was slowly letting music touch her deep inside. Letting it touch her and to release the pain that was destroying us. Every time a tear fell, it was pain being released. Music let her release that pain and it made her feel alive, too. She had no idea what was happening to her, she was extremely confused by the messages that both I and the **Saboteur** were throwing at her. I needed help in helping her. That damn school counselor was not quite the help I was looking for but it was a start, it was breathing room. Then came Michael and while the magic wand to give her a suddenly happy life was not waved, the healing process did begin. Her trek to live with the rest of the world began with the single sound of her voice. Finally the fragile person she was took the risk and said how badly she was hurt. I could not have saved us all by myself and Michael came just in time. The universe heard the cries and in he walked to comfort her and to be her friend, her brother, her protector, if only for a little while.*

*All is not completely peaceful here. Yes the tree and the meadow are beautiful now. The house I do not mind hanging out in, it's quite cozy but pain still lingers here. She still cries because there is so much more to be released, so much of the **Saboteur's** messages are still locked away in mental suitcases, slipping out now and then. There is a desperate need to fling the* *cases open and to cry, to let all that remains of the **Saboteur** to spill out and be released. It is that very reason that the need to be held remains so strong. It has been something since we were little that has stuck around. The need to come home from work, to lay down and have someone take us into their arms and for an hour or so, no words spoken but just the sounds of tears falling, being released and feeling vulnerable in the arms of another but yet feeling safe at the same time. There is no safe place for this to happen, there is no person available for her to be vulnerable to and yet feel safe. So silently we cry each night to ourselves, letting out the pain bit by bit in the hopes that one day we will no longer need to.*

Our world is content, ever the balancing trick as we sit on the wooden fence between the beautiful meadow and the darkened wasteland and forest. Here we sit, almost teasing Death to come get us again. Even with the medical problem we have plaguing us, we try as best as possible to live in this world, trying not to let it get the best of us. Once more we are fighting and it is the line from Highlander: The TV Series where Peter Wingfield who plays 'Methos' the five thousand year old immortal who says: "Live, grow stronger, fight another day."

That's exactly what we have been doing and will continue to do until the day we're really due to die and not a day before it.

CHAPTER FOURTEEN

"Miss You In A Heartbeat" – Def Leppard

The tentacles of depression and suicide cannot touch me like they used to. Yes, depression does grip me at certain times of the year for I miss friends long gone from my life. During these depressive times I mourn the loss of my friends, but I am also thankful for them having touched my life. I talk as if all my friends from my past are dead; they aren't. They might as well be since I don't know where any of them are. They say the friends you make in college remain with you for the rest of your life. That is half true. There are people from college I remain friends with but they are mostly what I call secondary friends. They aren't the people I hung out with all the time. They're more like the friends I saw once a week at the library, had class with, or worked at the radio station with, not the ones that I actually hung out with in their dorm room or anything. The friends I ate meals with and hung out will all the time, they are the friends I barely hear from anymore. There are two or three of that particular group that I'm in contact with on a regular basis but the friends that I really want to be connected to again are long gone from my life. It's for the best anyway. Can't keep living in the past but I guess that's why I sort of mourn for them in the fall. When September rolls around that's normally when I would be in school and going to classes and seeing my friends. I miss that. I miss that yearly reunion.

When fall comes around I get weepy, sentimental and go into reflective mode. I mourn for Michael. Maybe I mourn for the loss of myself. I celebrate October 14th which is the night Michael helped me and it is the day I began my transformation. I also celebrate November 1st as that is the day Michael died. There are other things that have happened in the fall, like my grandfather dying. I don't seem to mark his death; I just let it fly by. This might be due to the fact that I only saw my grandfather six times in my entire life and I wasn't all that close to him. I wasn't close to him like I was to Michael.

I probably sound obsessive about Michael. I can't help it. Michael was the guy that I wish I could come home to. He's the guy that I wish I could curl up with after long day of work and be vulnerable and safe with all at the same time. Michael is the very first guy that I have ever been honestly open with. He's the first guy that I ever told how I really felt inside. He's the first guy I ever really entrusted myself to. I guess he's the first guy I have ever really loved even if I didn't know it fifteen years ago. It wasn't until a few years ago that I realized that I loved him unconditionally.

We were very close friends and even though he helped me, he did some things that most people would have condemned him to a life of solitude

---

Journal Excerpt:
February 20, 2006

In our own twisted way we both found each other and gave the other life. His dark personality and lifestyle brought me into the light and I brought him with me. Two people in their own dark place finding refuge in one another. We made it though – we survived. Every obstacle that came at us we broke together, we became one in some ways. It was nice to have a brother if only for a short time. Maybe that's why it hurts to no longer have him around because he meant so much to me. I sometimes think I fool myself about him. Am I creating something that just wasn't there? I make Michael out to be this great guy, hiked up on a pedestal when in fact he doesn't deserve to be placed in such honor. Sometimes I think I give him too much credit for helping me. True, it was him that ignited something in me, woke me up and made me want to be alive. He gave me a reason to live but it was I who had to do all the work.

Michael caused me a lot of pain as well. I left college with regret on how our friendship ended. I still yearned for his attention but he didn't want to give it to me anymore. I carried a flame in my heart for him and still to this day it flickers. I loved him then and still do to this day. He hurt so many people in college including me but I was not the recipient of his vilest stuff. No, he let me be. He hurt me a little not a lot unlike the others that we hung out with. I was more forgiving than the others and I was the first to do so. If I bring his name up to others they scoff and say something nasty about him. Obviously time has not healed their wounds and it's true we all remember things differently.

I choose to remember Michael for the good stuff as well as the bad but there is no denying the others will never truly understand why he's so special to me. Maybe it's not meant for them to understand. Maybe Michael is my reminder that life can throw me lemons but eventually I'll make the lemonade, drink it and have a good time doing so.

for. I talked about Michael earlier but I guess it's time to take off the gloves and really expose him. He was a bad boy. Michael was an insensitive jerk, a trickster, a cheat, a con-artist in some cases.

I'm not sure which stories to tell about him for there were so many confusing things that he did. He surely did boggle the mind. So let me run down some of Michael's not so spectacular moments.

- Michael reportedly sleeps with Amy on Keira's (his girlfriend) birthday while she and I are in New Hampshire celebrating her twenty-first birthday with some of her high school friends. Keith is the one who spots Michael and Amy getting a little cozy in the main lounge and witnesses them disappearing.
- Michael hooks up with Jen who is a mutual friend of his and Keira's. Mind you Jen's a friend of mine, too. Michael and Jen have a romp in the hay which I suspect happened but can't confirm. I learn the truth after I graduate from college. However, Michael is not completely at fault as Jen was known to be a bit of a tramp. Michael was just another notch for her. Poor Keira never suspected a thing.
- Michael gets his girlfriend Keira pregnant and they head off to Connecticut for an abortion. Things go as planned but he ends up treating Keira like shit while she recovers from the procedure. He ends up practically ignoring her but for whatever reason Keira keeps dating him.
- Then there is the infamous trap in the theatre. It was an elaborate scheme to catch Michael cheating on Keira. There were several incidents that he had already but there was no proof. So the trap is set. Jen fakes getting a letter from her boyfriend that he no longer wishes to date her, Jen confides in Michael and he makes a move on her in the school theatre. Unknown to him, Keira is down below where he's sitting with Jen listening to everything. Across the stage is Dawn and Steve watching and listening and I'm also there watching and listening in between the stage curtains. Then the big explosion and Jen tells Michael no and out comes everyone. Keira rips him a new one and that's the end of that.
- Keira's teenage sister shows up unexpectedly at college and gives Keira a letter. In it, she tells Keira that Michael raped her when he was staying with them after his skiing accident where he broke his leg. Talk about a bombshell. By the way, no charges were ever filed against Michael.

Yeah folks, not the best guy in the world huh? Those were just a few of his not so best moments. You're probably wondering how I could have stayed friends with such a guy. To be honest I ask myself that same question sometimes but it all gets wiped away by the mere fact that he helped me. We all have bad parts of ourselves. Michael was no angel, but he showed me how to have a life again. He showed me how to live and for that I am ever grateful and all the bad that he did just doesn't seem to matter. Michael never did anything that directly hurt me. Sure, I didn't like the way he treated Keira and he knew that, too. When I would object to something he did, I simply stopped talking to him. It would take him a day or so to figure it out but I knew my silence hurt him. He probably never would have admitted it but he needed me just as much as I needed him.

The strange thing is as I think back he never ever apologized to anyone except Keira and me. I don't know why just us either.

Michael confided in me on a few occasions. There was the night that he told me in confidence that he had been institutionalized. He didn't tell me what for or how long, he just confided in me that he had been and I was the only one who knew. I kept that secret all the while we were at school but Keira knew that Michael had confided in me about something and it would later come back at him.

I'm not sure what happened exactly but I remember some big blow up going on between him and Keira. I can't recall how I was involved, but I remember heading back to my room and listening to Keira lay into him in my suite lounge. He was apologizing to her but she told him she didn't need the apology, I did. I was carrying his secret and he owed me an apology. The thing was Michael couldn't recall what he had shared with me and actually asked me what it was that he told me.

So I had to tell Michael outside my room late at night what he had confided in me. I remember crying when I told him because I felt betrayed for some reason. My memory is fuzzy about this incident but I do know when I told Michael what it was he told me, he hugged me and I cried and said goodnight to him. When I walked into my room my roommate and her boyfriend were asleep, or so I thought but her boyfriend had heard the whole conversation and ended up giving me a hug and asking if I was okay.

I think it was the night Keira broke up with Michael that this happened because shortly after it was agreed by all of Michael's friends at the time that we would ignore him, never talk to him again, and never do anything again with him. Like a fool I went along with the crowd because even though I was better, being accepted was something I still craved. I went along with my friends while my heart just broke. I couldn't understand why Michael had done the things he'd done to Keira because the Michael I knew was so warm and caring.

I would be with the gang walking across campus and spot Michael and while everyone else ignored him, I would watch him, casting a smile his way if he looked. When I hung out with my friends at first it was nothing but Michael bashing sessions and after awhile I just drowned it all out. I was with Keira when her sister showed up to tell her about the rape and I was floored. I guess my mind was trying to figure out how a guy in a leg cast could rape a sixteen year old while his girlfriend is just a few rooms away.

It's not that I didn't think it could happen, I just couldn't imagine Michael being that vile of a guy.

Journal Excerpt:
January 20, 2006

Maybe I think of Michael so much because I'm looking for clues. What was it about him that was so easy for me to open up to? I didn't know him very well. He was practically a stranger to me but it was so easy to talk to him. Maybe part of me thought I was talking to Death. Michael was something that I found, something that I had lost at some point and could never find when I needed it until that moment on October 14, 1992. There's the saying "Don't know what you got until it's gone" and the sad thing is I never knew what was gone. I never knew I had lost something as I never had it to begin with. That was Michael. He was something I had lost and then suddenly found. Except I didn't know I had lost him only because I didn't know I had him to begin with. I had it, lost it and found it again. I simply found Michael. Two strangers in pain who find themselves and come out of the dark, two strangers who learn to live again, two strangers who learn to love unconditionally. Two strangers who hurt each other, laughed together, cried together, smiled together. Two strangers who ended things badly with one another, two strangers far apart in the world, one full of regret, the other no cares in the world. Two strangers, one now dead, the other a survivor. Two strangers, for all time, locked together in memory and heart. Two strangers who are never two but always one.

I went through a lot with Michael, a lot of good and bad stuff and it's the good stuff that I really remember. Believe me, I have not forgotten the bad stuff but it's irrelevant to me. What matters is what he did for me, what we did together. For two people who didn't date each other or hang out twenty-four hours a day we were like brother and sister. We were a couple, our past lives intertwined with the present and karmic debts paid for. There's a line in a Def Leppard song that goes, "We were always the better part of me." Every time I hear that line I think of Michael because he really was the better part of me and thanks to him I'm still here. It's almost poetic that he died in 1999 waiting for a heart transplant.

CHAPTER FIFTEEN

"There's Still Time To Change The Road You're On" – Led Zeppelin

My transformation from the dark to the light has not been an easy one. Obviously *Inner Me* was quite busy trying to keep me alive but I was so sucked into killing myself that I was missing some signs. All of us have things that we are drawn to for some reason, perhaps past life memories. Who can really say? Do we really know how our inner self works or our brain? As I began this project certain things started to surface. I know that Steve Clark and Def Leppard have been a constant in my life and as it turns out there have been some other influences along the way. Some have stayed with me for years, some have come and gone.

I believe that our dreams hold keys to our journey and how we are progressing in understanding ourselves and changing who we are. They illuminate how we solve problems and grow from them. There are answers in our dreams that sometimes take a while to understand. More importantly, there are chances to talk to parts of ourselves to experience revelation. In dreamland, we are able to give voice to parts of ourselves we normally don't. People, places and things in dreams all mean something.

As I opened the gates to my past and awoke the darkness that has been dormant for so long, my dream world exploded too. Once more, I am sixteen years old waiting behind a barricade for Def Leppard to exit the arena I had just watched them play in. I'm surrounded by other fans but unlike them I'm quiet and not yelling when I see the band come out. I see Steve and lock right on him and he locks onto me. The rest of the members of the band come to the barricades but Steve's face suggests that if he approaches I'll be swallowed by the crowd. He talks to a security guard who comes to the barricade, helps me over it and escorts me to Steve. Steve smiles as I follow him onto the band's tour bus.

I sit down at a table as Steve prepares to make tea for us. Once it's ready he places a mug in front of me and sits down across from me. There is a moment of silence between us and then he starts to ask me questions.

"You play the guitar don't you?" "Yes."
"You're in a band, right?" "Yes."
"Dad yell at you?" "Yes."
"Makes you feel like nothing?" "Yes."
"Tried to kill yourself? "Yes."

He says he understands me and I tell him that I understand him. He quotes Led Zeppelin and tells me "There's still time to change the road you're on." I tell him there's still time for him to change his road but he says it's too late. We see the rest of the band approaching the bus when he asks me if I promise to be there for the guys the way they have been there for me. I make a promise to Steve that I will be there for the guys. I tell him that he inspires me, that the reason why I didn't succeed in taking my own life was because of him and the band.

He reaches across the table and places his hand on top of mine. I tell him that he makes me want to live but I don't know how. He stands up and motions for me to do the same. He then hugs me and whispers in my ear, "you will, you'll find your way." We both cry as he asks me one more time not to forget him. I tell him that I won't ever forget him and he tells me that he'll always be with me and "thank you for never giving up on me."

He finally asks me my name so I tell him it's Maynard and my last name is Clark. He chuckles as we keep holding each other. Then the door to the bus opens as the guys start to get on. Steve doesn't introduce me to them. He walks me to the door and reminds me what we talked about, "You'll find the road you need to be on and you'll learn how to live." One last time he hugs me and then off the bus I go, only to stand there and watch the bus drive off.

Aren't our dreams funny? It's almost like two time lines meet in this dream. It's as though I represent Steve when he was younger and to me he is what I could become which I think explains why he says the Led Zeppelin line to me. That's there's still time to change the road I'm on. It's too late for him but not for me. I still have a chance.

There are so many other musicians, bands, actors and athletes that speak to me in some way. There are also symbols and cultural signatures that get my attention. There are things my friends don't know about me as I've kept it secret but I'll share with all of you.

I like Celtic knots and things that are Celtic in nature including music. I have an odd fascination with Ireland and the Isle of Skye. Just saying the name of either place makes me long for home. I don't know how to explain that. Even seeing pictures induces that feeling of homesickness in me. One day I'll get there.

I have this fascination about King Arthur and Merlin and other people or stories, like Star Wars which have characters that can be traced to King Arthur and Merlin. I like some Native American and Oriental art, depending on what it is. So yeah, Celtic items are number one with me followed by Native American and Oriental art which strike me as beautiful and fascinating.

I do enjoy crows and ravens, and in some ways still have a fascination about Death. I guess my view of the world has changed from my depressive suicidal death march to a more contented view of things.

Other things that I'm into are things of a paranormal nature. I haven't channeled or played with the Ouija board in ages and on occasion I manage to dust off my automatic writing skills. I have to admit that I have an interest dealing with the otherworld, Spirits, Angels, Archangels, Druids and Pagans. I know that this stuff is taboo to some people, especially those brought up on a strict religious upbringing. While I did grow up Catholic and attended classes to be a good little Catholic, it never really sank in. The funny thing is all of the holidays like Halloween, Christmas and Easter that are observed are rooted in Paganism, so for me I'm a mish mash of it all.

For myself, I sit on a fence between the beautiful meadow and the dark swamp and forest. I'm comfortable on this fence for one side is dark and the other light. I see this fence as a nice place to sit, balancing the world and all that it is. On this fence I am a survivor and have been surviving as best as I know how for a long, long time. On this fence I see both sides of a lot of topics, just soaking it all in.

For a long time I didn't pay attention to the world around me, not that I've gotten extremely better about that but I am more aware. There are just so many unexplainable things that happen to us. Things we see and hear we often just shrug off when really we need to embrace it.

CHAPTER SIXTEEN

"It's Just An Angel Whose Wings Hide The Sun" – Def Leppard

Death always walks with me and I don't fear him. He's a rather cool guy to be quite honest. I'm not lying. After all the attempts I've made I would have been surprised if I hadn't met him. I think people misunderstand Death. There's Death and then there's death. I'm not talking about 'what a horrible death' meaning someone died tragically, I mean Death as in the dude in the black cloak, the one commonly known as the Grim Reaper or for those biblically minded folks, the Shadow of Death. Shadow sounds much nicer to call him anyway instead of Death. I suppose Shadow could be a woman but to me, no way. Shadow is a guy all the way, definitely a male persona.

In case you're wondering what Shadow looks like, he looks like you and me. That's assuming your idea of what Death looks like should be that. What I mean to say is that Shadow appears to you in the most comfortable form. So if for you, Death looks like a hot college student in tight jeans with an athletic build and blues eyes then that's what Death will look like to you.

Journal Excerpt:
February 20, 2006

When death gets close to your life it can shake you a bit. Sometimes it scares you and sometimes you find peace with it. There was a time when I was scared but when you get eerily close to ending your life you're not scared. You almost welcome it because there is this stillness, this peace you have never felt and maybe in that moment of clarity you understand that death is not a bad thing, it's a signal of the life cycle. In that moment you also realize that maybe you do have another chance. That you can make some correction to the line you are following. I can only speak from my point of view as someone who has made attempt after attempt to end their life.

If you think Death looks like an eight year old girl with pigtails wearing a pink dress, then you guessed it…that's what Death with look like. I think that's the coolest part of Shadow. That he or she, whichever the case may be, arrives in a form that is comfortable to you.

Shadow appeared to me one night as a gargoyle. He then changed his appearance to the more traditional black robe and hood, then more of human form but for the most part the black robe thing was okay for me. The scythe was left at home in case you're wondering. I may view him in a traditional sense but not that traditional. I wasn't scared of him but rather curious about him.

I brought up Death to Michael one night, asking if he'd ever seen him and Michael told me that he had. I asked him what he looked like and Michael proceeded to tell me he kind of looked like a cross between a gargoyle and a gremlin.

Journal Excerpt:
February 1, 2006

Michael has been dead for years but he's still alive for me and I'm not sure why. It's not like he can call me on the phone or send me an email message so why do I consistently put myself through this? True, I miss him but one would think that I would have finished mourning him awhile ago, if anything I should be celebrating him, honoring him which is what I do sometimes. I have lost a good friend and perhaps part of me does not wish to lose him for good. I'll always have my memories of him but as I said he's very much alive in me and I don't want to, for lack of a better choice of words, "kill him off." Even as I write this a tear formed in my eyes. Good gosh. How does the saying go? It's better to have loved and lost than never to have loved at all. I loved Michael, took me 13 years to figure it out with a little help from Naomi. I would never have said that I unconditionally loved Michael but looking back on things, I guess I did. So I have loved and have lost since well, Michael's dead and if I put him out of my head and think only of him once in a great while, then I have truly lost and it will feel like I never loved at all. It will feel like no one ever loved me when I know at least one person has.

It's strange. I can talk about my Grandpa K and Uncle Gilbert (may they rest in peace) and not shed a tear but talking about Michael gets me teary-eyed. Sometimes a tear will fall when I talk about him or I completely break down. He made me feel like a whole person and without him around I feel like I'm missing part of myself. Like he took a part of me with him and forgot to give it back.

I looked at Michael in amazement because I had viewed Death in pretty much the same way. Michael also did not fear Shadow. Through my transformation and all my experiences with the Ouija board, Shadow had actually become more like a friend and protector for us. He was our go-to guy when we really wanted to know something about the other side but for the most part we asked him what it was like to be him, to do what he did. How often is Shadow asked for a job description? I always sensed that he was flattered that we would take the time to ask him about himself. Seriously, we're so wrapped up in ourselves that he probably is hardly ever asked about himself. It was a good experience all the way around.

I think knowing Shadow the way that I did made things easier to deal with. When my grandfather died, I was the only one smiling at the church service and at the cemetery. I just imagined my grandfather sitting in his boat catching fish, having a grand time while everyone else were crying their eyes out. Maybe I didn't get so darn emotional because I had only seen my grandfather six times in the thirty years I'd been alive. I wasn't close to him like everyone else. He lived in South Dakota and I lived in Vermont, so it wasn't easy to visit him.

When my uncle passed away it was the same situation as was with my grandfather, but I wasn't able to go to South Dakota for his funeral because it was the middle of winter. I didn't get upset that he died, either, as he'd been sick for a long time. The only person that I have gotten upset about dying was Michael.

I had lost touch with Michael for many years. While searching for him on the internet I found a tribute page for him. There on the page in front of me were a couple of pictures and an explanation of what caused his death.

I contacted the person who owned the page and she told me how she visited Michael in the hospital and that he had mentioned me. Out of all the people from college he only mentioned me. I found out about Michael's death in 2001, learning that he died in 1999.

For years something plagued me about his death. Finally in 2005 I couldn't take it anymore, and I went on a search to know the real truth about Michael's death because the story I had gotten bothered me. I went looking for truth and then found it. Michael didn't die from the asthma medication he was on; no, he died as a result of waiting for a heart transplant. Also, he wasn't in Boston when he died; he was in Connecticut. So yeah, why would someone tell me some fake story about an old friend? I don't know but it hurt me a lot when I learned the truth. I cried really hard but yet felt at peace knowing the truth about Michael. I contacted Michael's parents, but never heard from them. At least they know that their son did something really wonderful when he helped me.

Here I am talking about Michael when I'm supposed to be talking about Shadow. Ugh. I guess it's because I equate Michael with Shadow. I equate him with Death. I know, why would I equate someone who was a very important part of my life with Death? Well, that's rather easy to explain. Michael looked like Death! I kid you not. Michael always wore a black trench coat (long before Keanu Reeves made it cool to wear one), had black sunken eyes, and wasn't merely ghostly pale; he was a block of ice in Antarctica kind of pale, igloo pale, north pole pale. Catch my meaning? I lived so long in the dark that seeing someone like Michael, or Shadow for that matter didn't bother me. You know what they say, misery loves company. Who was I to toss away a potential friend or two? I'm sure not a lot of people would pick Death to be their best buddy, but as I mentioned before, he seemed okay to me. Shadow wouldn't get angry or overly happy, he was very even emotionally and he sure as hell didn't spew out angelic witticisms or wise proverbs from some ancient time. Shadow was Joe Average with a wicked sense of humor. When it came to scaring people he was really good at that too. Both Michael and I knew when he was up to no good and was about ready to scare someone. It was just hard to sit there and not laugh or give away what was about to happen but once it did, Michael and I would just lose it.

I suppose that since I hung out with Michael, who was someone who went through his own dark times, and then throw in Shadow, it makes sense that I view death and dying from a unique point of view or perhaps I don't. I just think when people fear dying too much, that they will miss out on something. They will miss out on the beauty of what it is. Shadow once told me that he's only as strong as the world wants him to be. When ninety-five percent of the world population is scared of dying, of Death in general, it's not hard to see what he means. He's part of the universal conscious. He'll continue to exist only because people want or need him to.

I'm glad he's so entwined with the universal conscious because if there was no Shadow then things would be a bit boring I think. I mean, I never would have met him for starters. There's a ton of stuff I would never have learned if it hadn't been for him. For instance, I had no clue that he had assistants.

He's like Santa but with creepier looking elves and unfortunately no sleigh. He also doesn't hand out gifts although some might consider walking with him to their new destination a gift. People fear Shadow so much that they miss out on what could be something really good. People envision him to be this demonic creature when he's not.

Call me skewed if you will but I guess because of what I've been through, I've seen and experienced that Shadow isn't scary after all. It's actually pretty nice that someone shows up when you die. Imagine if you die and no one is there to greet you or walk with you or tell you anything. With Shadow being there at least you have someone to help you get a grip with what happened to you and be by your side as you make the adjustment from living to dead. Then again, just because your physical body is kaput doesn't mean you are, does it? You continue on long after your physical body, so in a sense you're immortal. (There can be only one! - Highlander fans will get that.)

A message from Shadow:
November 20, 2005

Of all the people I've met through the centuries, you are the only one I know who celebrates their survival date. I was there for your party with your friends this year. I know that October 14th, 1992 is the last time you tried to take your own life and to mark such a date with your friends was something very special. When you lit your candle and your friends lit theirs in remembrance to friends past and present it sent a wonderful ripple of love around. You are a survivor, kiddo. Everyday that you get up and face the world is another day you survive. - Shadow

---

I think we all mourn for different reasons and I have been mourning Michael for a long time. When October 14th and November 1st roll around, I light a candle in honor of myself and for Michael. It is an acknowledgement that I have not forgotten him and will always remember our friendship. For the past few years I have given my closest friends candles on October 14th. I do this so they can light the candle to reflect and be thankful for the friends they have now, the friends they once had and the friends they have yet to meet. I think we all forget to honor our friends and just simply lighting a candle in honor of all the people who have helped us over the years is a nice gesture. It is a symbolic gesture. One that makes us more aware of the people we surround ourselves with, the people we call our friends.

CHAPTER SEVENTEEN

"I Walk Alone In The Darkness Of The City" – Richie Sambora

When I sat down to write about my suicide years, originally I was going to write a fictional story loosely based on me. I had character names and a general outline of where I wanted the story to go but when I sat down to write, I knew that I couldn't fictionalize this. I needed to be open about it for myself.

I have written all of this from my point of view and from *Inner Me* and the **Saboteur's** view, too. Like any good writer I consulted three of my friends to come up with some things I may have neglected to write about when I began spewing out my rambled thoughts. I will readily admit that three of these questions made me laugh but I'm not going to tell you which ones. Why I laughed, I'm not sure. I think it's because I'm so comfortable with my suicide years to an extent that some of them just seemed funny. By no means is suicide something to laugh about; it's just that I view it differently fifteen years removed from my last attempt.

As far as answering these questions, I'll do my best to answer them and most likely *Inner Me* and the **Saboteur** will chime in for some of them. Seems only fair they speak too. So without further adieu, welcome to the Q & A section!

1) Why didn't the suicide "attempts" work?
Well, it wasn't due to a lack of trying. Let's see, I tried to light myself on fire once. That didn't work because I couldn't actually get my shirt to light. It's not easy holding a lighter and trying to get the shirt you're wearing to burn. It's really hard to do especially in the dark! So I kind of gave up on that one. After that, several attempts with alcohol followed by extra-strength Tylenol chasers only left me crying, shaky, desperate feeling and bed ridden. There was the night with the plastic knife across my wrists. In case you're wondering, plastic knives are sharp. I managed to do both wrists, but not

enough to do any serious damage. You can't even see my scars anymore but I know they're there. They are always visible to me. So, I did the act but the finale sucked. I was either too drunk or not drunk enough to be successful. Surely I can't forget my roof incidents either. As much as I looked over the edge I never made it up on the ledge because ironically enough I have a problem with heights. I mentioned it earlier but I'll mention it here again that only my very first attempt and my last attempt I was sober for. For everything else, I was drunk.

Her attempts didn't work because she's a failure. Dumb bitch tried but she sucked on the follow through. Execution was stellar but the rest was a disgrace and at times somewhat humorous.

*Her attempts didn't work because I was battling you, **Saboteur**. A few times you almost had her but I wasn't willing to give up so easily. You were so blind to the fact that I was using music to keep her alive. Music heals us in many ways, on many different levels and all I can say is thank goodness for Def Leppard. Thank goodness for them until Michael and Keith arrived into her life.*

2) How come you didn't use a method that would <u>for sure</u> get the job done?
Well, I didn't have access to a gun to put a bullet in my head and I didn't own a car so I couldn't fulfill the usual cheap cliché of driving off a cliff. I also didn't own a big ass knife and there was nothing on my dorm room ceiling that I could have hung myself from.

Ah, the sarcasm comes out. True, true you couldn't do those things. You forgot to mention that you sat outdoors in the middle of winter with no coat on for awhile in an attempt to freeze yourself. Except you were a big chicken and couldn't handle it. After ten minutes you were inside having chicken soup! You were so pathetic!

At least she was smart enough not to listen to you. Alcohol was very accessible to her so it was the natural choice to go and most people wouldn't think of a suicide right away. Most would have assumed she drank too much and died. Steve Clark died from drinking too much; he was an alcoholic and even though she wasn't one, she was getting there. That's why she identified with him back then and identifies with him now. In her mind, Steve understood her and she understood him. He validated her feelings.

3) How did you imagine the impact on your family, friends, or were you beyond thinking about it?

This is a really good question and honestly I can say that I didn't care too much. My thought patterns were so directed toward myself and the repeated message that no one will notice kept playing in my head. I was the invisible girl. If I died, no one would miss me, right? That's the mentality I had and I really didn't care what would happen to the people around me. I had a few friends who were concerned early on, but to be honest I didn't think of them. I guess my friendships with them weren't strong enough to actually keep me here. I was just pulling away in a sense. To be honest, nothing was keeping me here except a part of myself I wasn't listening to at the time. Many apologies to my *Inner Self.*

We were all alone for this journey. There was no one to support us and no one we thought we could confide in. We had friends who we showed glimpses of our pain to but not so much that they were aware of how much we hurt. We wore a mask as much as possible to hide it from everyone. We suffered in silence. We cried in silence. Sometimes we still do.

4) Were there things that you purposely did "for the last time" before your attempts?

Amazingly, no. I didn't clean my room or hand possessions off. Though I suppose you could argue that I left things alone as if it were a snapshot of the person I was. The only thing I did was type a short letter and stuck it to the inside of my desk hutch in the event I actually succeeded. It had instructions and contact information for my parents. So I guess part of me was concerned but obviously not THAT concerned. Every time I sat at my desk to do homework the letter was in plain sight so I guess it also served as a reminder of the confusion I was in.

Sure, usually a sign of someone being suicidal is that they give away their possessions. She didn't have many possessions to begin with so there was really nothing to give away. The intent was to die and get away from this world, to put her ugly ass six feet under and to put herself out of her misery. Then again, it was to put us out of our misery. I was driving the proverbial car as fast as I could and boy did I see a nice looking cliff coming up but damn *Inner Me* got in the way. Bastard.

As a child in many forms, I waver from being an eight year old to a sixteen year old and I find it almost humorous that you got beat by a kid. The right thing to do would have been to leave something behind for someone, but there was no one meaningful to give such tokens to. There was no one who influenced us or changed us, from a friend point of view anyway. She felt no self-worth and therefore her belongings had no worth and there was no one in her life that was worthy in her mind. Her world was full of fake views. She was searching for truth, for authenticity and all that was reflected back was false. Life was meaningless for her, for us. When you hurt this much, so much that you want to kill yourself, leaving notes and giving possessions away seems meaningless. They are empty actions in a seemingly empty and worthless life.

5) What did you learn about your real friends through it all?

I dealt with my depression and suicide attempts behind closed doors. I didn't share my feelings with anyone, really. I attempted to but it was obvious from the people who I called "friends" that they wouldn't be very understanding or supportive. I hurt a lot and I really needed to tell someone but there was no one to tell it to. I pretty much realized that the people I hung out with and ate lunch with were just friendly faces. I think my friends were still trying to discover themselves. Then again in college, just like high school, I was the invisible girl. People talked to me but because of my shy, introverted personality I wasn't screaming for attention even though I was trying to.

My "real" friends didn't show up until the final year of my depression and suicidal tendencies. That's when Michael and Keith popped up in my life. I had always known Keira but we just crossed paths a lot because we lived in the same dorm. I think we got to know each other better after her boyfriend got in her face way more than any guy should. We were friendly faces for a couple of years but it kept building because we were both studying communications and worked at the radio station. When Michael came along, so did Keira and Raine.

All of us were communications majors. I had originally started out in TV but switched to radio by my junior year. The others were all radio majors from the start. When the four of us came together, we weren't just classmates, we were friends. We had a shared passion for music and we had a shared interest in the paranormal. We were very much our own people individually but when we came together it felt like family.

You had sucky friends in the beginning. Who are you kidding? You never had any real friends. Everyone picked on you, even in college because you were so fucked up! You kept trying to make friends but it never quite worked the way you wanted. You were too emotional and too clingy and needy. The closer you tried to get to people the more they pushed you away. This, of course, helped me out tremendously when it came to reinforcing the fact that no one liked you and that you were an absolute zero, a nothing, a nobody.

Give her a break, will you? Making friends and trusting them was very hard for her, for us. She grew up in a neighborhood with no other kids around, she was shy and quiet and didn't have any siblings to talk to or help out with stuff. She didn't have anyone to confide in, it just remained inside her. She hadn't developed her skill for writing until high school and that's when she finally gave voice to what was inside. Writing is the one talent she had and still has. Making friends was hard because as much as she hung out with others she always felt uncomfortable. She felt she couldn't be who she really wanted to be and when she was authentic, she was ridiculed for it. She trusted no one. When you don't trust people, it's hard to open up to them whether they are a friend or not.

She got lucky with Michael, with Keith and the people she's met since then but back then making friends was torturous. It was much easier to be alone, which didn't help her at all. There was no such thing as a real friend back then. Even now she doesn't think the friends she has are real. They are real, but convincing her of that has been a struggle. For her it will always be baby steps when making friends and trusting them with whatever she may share with them. Everything that she has ever revealed about herself in the past has often resulted in her getting hurt. She's cautious at first and then opens up as time goes on. She's simply trying to protect herself, and that's why she's slow to trust people.

6) Do you ever think about suicide now? How do you take care of yourself?

Sure I think about it, but not with the intent to kill myself. There is a difference. There is a difference between thinking about it and thinking with the intent to actually do it. I think about my attempts, I reflect back on how I was because now that I'm removed from that part of my life I can look at it differently. Now that I'm older there are things I now see I never could have controlled. I also see that there was just no way for me to have dealt with everything any better than what I did. Seriously, no one was paying attention even when I gave them something to pay attention to. I just wanted to be seen and I suppose in some ways I was making attempts to get attention be-cause I needed someone to help me. It's hard to get help if everyone is look-ing the other way.

I used to have dreams where I killed myself. It was like I was trying to kill off parts of myself that just weren't needed or I didn't like. I was try-ing to find myself, who I was, the authentic me if you will. Buried under all this societal, parental garbage was someone who just wanted to be herself and not the good, little girl with the polite smile who stayed in line. I'm a nice person, but being the goodie-goodie was a very tiring act. I wanted to show more of who I was without being ridiculed.

Suicide will always be a part of me and yes, I will freely admit that there are times where it's on my mind for days. It's during those streaks that I desperately need a hug and most of all a person to rely on, but most of the time I rely on me. When I am down for days I am susceptible to crying practically on demand and the last place I want to be is at work but it's better to be at work than laying in bed with the blanket pulled over my head. During these streaks is when I really, really want to be held or hold onto someone for a long hug but you can't do those things at work – how unprofessional – yet I do get hugs, I just try my best to keep the tears in check.

As far as taking care of myself I just try and write in my journal everyday. I listen to music that I know makes me feel good or music that expresses how I feel. I make sure that behind closed doors I cry so as not to keep it in. I get tired when I get down so I sometimes go to bed a bit earlier and let my vivid imagination drift me off to sleep by imagining that I'm being held by someone. It sounds strange, I know. I am happy to report that this type of visualization is used by many people when they are very stressed or troubled. Basically one takes a few deep breaths, closes their eyes as they lay in bed and then imagines snuggling down into the Archangels Raphael's arms. While doing this you feel the warmth of his body, his arms and wings enveloping you with love. This really is a good exercise because you often get a good night of sleep plus, resting in his arms brings you peace, love and the feeling of security. I don't visualize Raphael very often, I actually think of my friend Michael, inviting him to spend time with me which he does. More often than not he brushes my face or says something nice and instantly I slip off to dreamland.

7) When you were depressed what changes in your life/circumstances did you envision that would have "fixed" everything?

That's easy, a boyfriend. Yup. I thought my answer to fixing myself was to have a boyfriend. Why? Well, let's see, (1) I would have worth. Someone wanted me. (2) I wouldn't be ignored and invisible. I would be seen and listened to. (3) I would be loved. Someone would give their heart to me and me to them. (4) Hugs. Yes, finally I would get those. (5) I would be pretty. In the sense that if I had a guy that meant I must be pretty and not ugly according to the many years of verbal assault my classmates lashed at me. (6) Happy. Hey, I would be happy and smile and frolic around about life.

There's a whole list but believe it or not I thought a boyfriend was the answer to all my problems. Seriously all I wanted was for someone to listen to me, hug me, hold me, care about me, and help me. I was looking for someone to help me be stable. The sad thing is these thoughts haven't gone away completely.

Having a boyfriend was a priority and I put so much emphasis on it that I destroyed that for myself. These days I could care less if I have a boyfriend or not but I DO care about having a male friend who I can be open with. Someone I can be myself with. No judgment, no ridicule, just be my friend, a guy to enjoy life's journey with, along with all the ups and downs that go with it. In other words, I need Michael or someone like him or even Keith. Those are my templates.

To not have either one in my life sucks. Michael is dead, and I know what you're thinking. What the hell is it with this Michael fellow? For once, all that I ever wanted I got because of Michael. Michael has been dead for eight years now and it hurts to not have him here. I mean he's here for me as I sense the comedic fool is around me sometimes but it's his physical form I miss. Kind of hard to hug a dead person, you know.

Keith is off in Florida and married to a wonderful woman named Julie which I am happy about. I'm glad he's doing well for himself. He went through a bad marriage and then a divorce after college so to know that he's happy is a good thing. Then again, that's all I ever want for my friends, to be happy.

I worry about my friends a lot because I want them to be happy and it sucks when they aren't. I tend to put other people first before myself, which is a problem. It might be a residual effect of me having been depressed and suicidal for so many years. I'm taking care of others long before I take care of me but I'm trying to be better about that. I feel guilty sometimes when I'm not "available" to help them out, though.

I know I tick my friends off when they want to do something and I'm just this boring girl who's a bit set in her ways. I can't help it, bars and places with tons of people annoy me. I like sitting somewhere (most of the time) at a table just hanging out. It's true. I'd rather be at home then running around all over town like a crazy person. Plus, my medical condition hinders me from having a somewhat normal life, so I'm always taking that into consideration.

My friends probably think I'm cold because they may tell me something bad, sad, glad whatever and I show almost no emotion, or if I do it's like I don't care. It's not that I don't care, it's just that I'm internally processing it. I'm feeling it on the inside and my mind is zooming about how I can fix the problem or how I can show my support. Then again, there are cases where I honestly just don't care, it's like "Why are you telling me this and what do you want me to do about it?"

It's bad to have that attitude and most of the time it's just people venting which is cool, I don't mind but sometimes I'm mentally thinking "shut up." That's me wanting to do my own thing and also a part of me learning to tune out, to not take it in and process it. I internalize a lot and I guess I'm still working on not taking everything in although it's been pretty damn hard not to do that.

I do show my emotions, but I guess I don't want people to make a big fuss sometimes. This is especially true when I do something nice for someone. I have problems accepting compliments or being thanked. For instance, I once gave a friend this wooden mosaic tray I had done. They went absolutely overboard about how much they loved it and blah, blah, blah it's so beautiful. I was like, whoa, pull back the reigns. It seemed so over the top to me that I actually wanted to take the gift back. A thank-you will suffice; I don't need a stage production to show me your appreciation.

As far as compliments go, this is a problem area for me as well. I don't accept them very well. Someone may tell me something is beautiful or I did a good job or I look nice today. To actually hear those sincere compliments is very hard. For a good chunk of my life when someone said "you look pretty" that translated into "you look ugly." I still get that mixed-up translation these days. I try to make sure "you look pretty" translates into "you look pretty" but it's not easy. I'm probably at the fifty-fifty stage when it comes to that. Accepting compliments is an on-going battle because a lot of time I hear the words, look at the person and then my mind thinks about it. Are they just saying it to say it or do they honestly mean it? We all do it; we say something just to be nice. I guess I'm always looking to see if the compliment was genuine or just some off-handed comment because it was the right thing to say.

8) Did you explore all avenues prior to your attempts, i.e. therapy? hospitalization? And if not, then why?

No, I didn't explore avenues for help because I wasn't sure just what was wrong with me. In high school and in college I thought I was doing okay on my own trying to deal with it. One of my friends tricked me into seeing the school counselor for therapy which was sort of a waste of time. I did have friends who thought I needed to be hospitalized after a night of using the Ouija board.

I guess part of me thought I could fix myself on my own. You have to remember I didn't have any help from my parents. They were emotionally unavailable to me. I had to do things for myself and this was just something else that I was doing for myself. I didn't know how to get better, I was too upset but *Inner Me* was doing the best it could considering how fragile and weak we were.

CHAPTER EIGHTEEN

"Livin' Is The Best Revenge You Can Play" – Def Leppard

One question that pops up is how did I recover from my depression and suicide? I'm not sure if I recovered in the way one thinks of recovery. It's more like survival.

Recover my ass. What? Do you think she's all better? Hell, no. You people like to fool yourselves all the time. A lot of you are wandering around feeling like crap but you pretend that all is right in the world.

*I have to partly agree with the **Saboteur**. I cannot say that we are recovered in the sense of getting over a cold but more like the destructive part is dormant. It's a part of who we are and it will never go away. It can resurface and take control at anytime. That destructive part – the **Saboteur**, is only as strong as the power we give it. This is a constant battle and at certain times of the year it's an all out war not to give in to the **Saboteur**. It's been fifteen years since the last attempt to kill ourselves so things are good for the most part. You can't simply recover from suicidal tendencies. It takes time and strength and an underlying belief in oneself to transform. Take what's negative and make it positive somehow because your life depends on changing your thought patterns. It's not easy at all. There's no magic wand to make all the pain go away and the next day you're instantly happy. It doesn't work that way at all. You fight, you struggle, you claw your way to a better place and hope that someone is there for you, to help you up off the ground when you've finally crawled out from the dark pit of pain. There is no such thing as instant happiness, you cannot bottle it, for it's an emotion that comes and goes just like any other. The object is to experience life with more happy moments than sad ones. The transformation from dark to light is painful in its own way because you're trying to break free of bad patterns, trying* *to rewrite them in a way that is more beneficial to who you are and who you become.*

Everyday I look in the mirror and for the longest time I hated who I saw. I still see my old self, though my face doesn't show the pain like it used to but I know it's still there. People often wonder how I could have been suicidal because I seem rather happy a lot of the time. I guess I rely on the things I know like covering up how I really feel. When I was depressed the one emotion I never showed was anger. It wasn't until I started transforming myself that anger showed up. What had been internalized was now externalized and in some way by doing that, the **Saboteur** wasn't as powerful anymore. I took control of the proverbial car.

There are some days where I don't want to drive. I'd rather pull over to the side of the road and take a nap. I'd rather go to some place nice with a big kick ass bed and some wonderfully pleasant guy I know or don't know is there, waiting to take care of me. I've been taking care of myself since I was a kid. In some ways I never got to be a kid, in the way a kid should be.

My parents neglected me, forcing me to take care of myself. They were emotionally unavailable so I had to do the best I could with what I had, which wasn't much. Seriously my parents were so unavailable that they never read me stories before bed or even tucked me in. I had to tuck myself in when I was kid!

I had no templates to look at to know how I was supposed to be. I had to look around me and to be honest there wasn't much for me to see. I ran away from home when I was ten years old, just a fifth grader and the one place I ran to was school after hours. Guess what? My parents didn't even know I had taken off; they assumed I was playing in the park behind our house. My mom of all people should have known something was up when she saw me packing my blanket into a back pack! I didn't stay away from home too long; the excursion lasted all of three hours. I just needed to get out of the house and away from them.

I suppose I could have been depressed as a kid. It stands to reason that I was and Middle School started to bring it out, High School heightened it more and college just overwhelmed me to the point that I was a ticking time bomb waiting to self-destruct. I basically gave in to the pain that I had been trying to keep tucked away but it was just too much and I let the **Saboteur** take control of the car completely.

How I got control of the car back, I'm not really sure. I probably pulled over to the side of the road, told *Inner Me* to get into the backseat with the **Saboteur** and let them go at it while Michael taught me how to drive. Once I was good at driving the car he let go and got out of the car. I suppose that's how you could look at it. I also look at it from a stand point that he helped me pick up my sword, the sword we all carry in ourselves, the sword that helps us fight and cut away unnecessary strings of pain. Michael gave me the sword and Keith is the one who taught me how to use it. Swords are heavy and driving a car for a long period of time can make one rather tired. Some days I just want to lay down the sword or pull the car over and take a rest, it depends on which metaphor you wish to use. It's when I feel tired or need a rest that the **Saboteur** looks to drive the car. I can't have the **Saboteur** drive the car but I wish some nice person would drive my car for me now and then. Come to think of it, I let Michael drive my car a time or two because I think he knew I needed to rest but also because I trusted him with my life. No one has ever driven my car but me since him.

Part of me accepts what has happened to me. There's nothing I can do about it; what's done has been done but there is a part of me that is angry. I guess I get angry when people comment that I don't seem like my normal self. Of course, to most of these people they don't know of my past so they have no idea what I've been through. I just want to go off and get in their face about it. Believe me folks, there is this rant in my head full of anger and pain. No matter how I explain what life was like for me back then some people don't get it unless I go over the top about it. So for your reading pleasure, and I apologize for the lack of popcorn for this but nonetheless, I present to you my suicidal rant.

***

Fifteen years have gone by since my last attempt. Do you think it's easy for me now? It isn't. Every day is a struggle to keep my ass here, in this place. It's never ever easy for a suicide survivor to continue on. No matter how many years pass between attempts or when things seem better the darkness always calls.

I'm still trying to help myself, damn it. You think I woke up one morning all cheerful and shit? I hate to tell you, but the transformation from depressed to happy didn't happen overnight. There was no fucking magic wand to make all the pain go away. Every damn day I have to look at myself in the mirror I still see her, you know. The person I once was. I still see her, she hasn't gone away. She's not on vacation. She is right here. She's a part of me. Don't you understand that there is no such thing as instant happiness? Not for someone like me. It doesn't work that way. It never will. Just because I haven't tried to kill myself in fifteen years doesn't mean my life is perfect. I made the mistake of thinking if my life was happy then I could have all the things I ever wanted. Believe me I learned quickly that it doesn't work that way because if it did, someone would hug me every now and then. A simple hug, is that too much to ask for? Some kind of acknowledgement is all I ever wanted from anyone. The problems I had fifteen years ago didn't vanish from my life, they're still here and I'm still trying to fix them. Everyone around me is more advanced than I am. I'm trying to make up for lost time for the seven years of my life I wasted on depression and suicide. Seven years! Seven long painful years!

Don't think I don't feel the darkness reaching out to me now and then, inviting me to come back to it. The scary thing is I sometimes want to. I know that I don't ever want to be that way again, depressed and suicidal. I don't want to be that way again but it hasn't been easy being in the happy realm either. There is still a lot of stuff I don't have or know how to get for myself.

Michael was not the last person for me to love; there will be another someday. There will be a day where someone will want to hold my hand and walk down the street with me, or sit at the local ice cream shop and eat ice cream with me. There will be a day where I can hang out with a friend who will hold me while I watch a movie or a time when I can come home or go to someone else's home and fall asleep knowing that I'm safe. I've wished for these things for a long time and I'm still alone. I give a lot to my friends, I make sure they're okay but it's such a one way street sometimes. I wonder a lot when someone will take care of me so I can rest. I'm so tired, so very tired. Every person who spends each day fighting for survival gets tired after a while. Every warrior needs a day of rest and I'd really like to know when mine is.

I hurt everyday but I know that I'm strong enough that darkness cannot take me. It will never take me again. I have to keep fighting for what I have and what I want no matter how much I hurt and no matter how much I want to give in sometimes. It took me a long time to learn that no one can help you unless you help yourself. Until that happens, you won't see happiness or hope, you won't know love and certainly won't know your own worth.

***

I hope my over the top rant helped shed some more light on what it's like to battle depression, suicide and yourself. Sometimes you just have to go over the top to get a point across.

CHAPTER NINETEEN

"Long, Long Way To Go" – Def Leppard

Fifteen years seems like a long time, but not to me. Not when I think about my attempts or how I used to be and in some aspects how I still am. It seems like only yesterday that it all happened. It seems like only yesterday that Michael and I had lunch together and enjoyed a few laughs. In my mind I saw Keith yesterday as well, along with Keira and Raine. In my mind I saw myself as well, vulnerable and lost, yet stable.

Sometimes I think I haven't gotten better at all, that depression still has me, it's just that I'm not as bad as I used to be. Perhaps I'm on some different level of depression. I don't think about killing myself but I do think about that time of my life. Searching for some clue or something that I can correct to make how I live and feel now, better. I search for an understanding of why I was depressed and suicidal. I look to this dark time in my life and keep learning from it, learning why something may have helped me but I was so lost that I couldn't see it. For instance the importance music had on my life.

In writing about my attempts and going through my old high school journals, I noticed that when I mentioned music it was mostly Def Leppard. I had no idea back then that their music mattered so much to me. I really didn't. It wasn't until I was working on another writing project that the importance of music surfaced. While working on that project and figuring out the artwork I wanted to include, Steve Clark came to mind and then Def Leppard's music ran through my head. It's like in that moment I unlocked something that I had forgotten I knew. I tapped into a deeper knowledge of some sort and that's when I realized just how important Steve Clark and Def Leppard were to me. I realized how much their music spoke to the deeper part of me.

My life is not sunshiny perfect by any means. I go to work, I go home, I sleep and do it all again the next day. My friends are few and even with the amount that I have, I sometimes feel like I don't have any. I do enjoy spending time with my friends, but I think because I am an only child it's sometimes difficult spending more than two to three hours with them because I just have this overwhelming desire to be by myself.

It's actually what happens when I get home everyday. After being at work all day and riding the bus home surrounded by people, I get home, change my clothes and lock myself away in my room to basically decompress. Needing time alone is a daily thing and very necessary for me. It's how I recharge myself, how I reset myself. As much as I crave to have someone in my life, at the same time I pull away from people. I'm a yo-yo.

I know that part of the reason I don't get close to people is because I need alone time and being surrounded by someone for long periods of time bugs the hell out of me. I think that's why I had boyfriend problems in college. I couldn't get away from my boyfriend for he was always there and I needed to get away. Basically what would have worked was a, "don't come to me, let me come to you," situation. It's really shitty to do that to someone but it's how I am. I'm not sure how I can fix it per se, except if I'm ever with someone again I'll explain that I need me time.

This may also tie into the fact that I don't want to get married. I see it as a hassle and if I'm married to someone, how the hell do I get away from them? I think that's why for me, finding someone to enjoy the journey with, a very close friend I can get together with now and then and hang out at a diner for a meal sounds like a good thing. Someone I can hang out with and open up to like I did with Michael and sort of with Keith. I loved the times I went out with Keith to the Miss Caledonia diner for hot chocolate. It was always spontaneous and the time spent with him was quiet and fun.

I miss those times. I miss those kinds of activities where it's ten p.m. and I'm out having a late night ice cream or snack with a good friend. Even the occasional dinner or lunch is fine, too. I think I have problems with parties and crowds because I've always hated being surrounded by that many people. It's overwhelming for me. It's like my brain gets overloaded with all the sounds getting thrown at me. I basically blow a circuit you could say. I'm just a highly sensitive person. Since I'm a loner, I have difficulty getting to know people. This is something I think I'm getting better at but I'm such an observer in a group setting that getting me to jump out of my comfort zone is a bit tough. I will admit that I'm not as quiet as I used to be. I think once I got through my depression and suicide and basically found a bit of stability for myself that my confidence grew as well. I'm still timid and shy in certain situations, but I try to fit in for the most part. That's an issue too. Part of me just wants to fit in all the time but that's something that got me into trouble to begin with.

It's not easy breaking old patterns and I know that I can't fix them all at once. I know that all I can ask of myself is to change things at my own speed and to heal myself the only way I know how.

To heal I need to continue making time for myself, writing and listening to music. I need to do things that I enjoy like making my greetings cards, crafts and also do things that I enjoyed as a kid, like pastel drawing.

Hopefully one day I'll find that person to enjoy the journey of life with. Someone I can curl up with on a couch and watch a movie with, someone who will accept me for who I am. They say your friends are a reflection of yourself and if that's the case I have nice, fun, vibrant, colorful friends. They show all the parts of me I have yet to show on my own.

Suicide is not a laughing matter and anyone who has thought about it, know that what you feel is okay. Having those thoughts doesn't make you mentally ill. People who think that way are uninformed. A few months back a guy was standing on the ledge of one of the parking garages near where I work. When I learned that there was a guy there wanting to jump I felt sad for him. I wanted to go find him and tell him I understood. I was at work when I found out the news and one of my co-workers automatically labeled the guy as insane. Hearing them say that hurt me. They didn't stop there either, they made all these comments and then eventually I did the one thing I normally don't do. I went into their office and told them point blank that I had once been suicidal and labeling this person in crisis as insane was unfair.

Listening to them label this poor guy as insane felt like they were saying I was too. You don't know what it's like unless you've been there yourself, and obviously my co-worker had never been in such a situation as to contemplate killing their self.

I didn't get an apology from my co-worker and to be honest I wasn't expecting one. All I hope is that my co-worker realized that they shouldn't jump so quickly to think someone that distressed was mentally ill. When I was in the depths of darkness, gripped hard in suicide I had friends actually laugh at me because they thought the reasons I wanted to kill myself were silly. Looking back, sure, some of those things were silly but the point is I needed their support and not their biting verbal assaults filled with laughter.

Wanting to kill yourself is hard to deal with. Just making that decision is not an easy thing to do. The last thing you want is to reach out for help and be denied by those closest to you. In college I had a few friends who did just that; they turned away from me. When your support system turns on you it only reinforces the bad things you feel already. Wanting to kill yourself can be an act of getting attention, but it's an act of desperation mostly because you're trying to get attention, some way some how. You're trying to get someone, anyone to see you and hear you. The problem is if you believe that no one cares for you, then it seems like no one will see you at all. The feeling of being invisible becomes severely exaggerated.

I don't have all the answers. I'm not all knowing but I know what it's like to be in a place that's dark and full of despair. I know what it's like to feel unloved, unwanted and invisible. I know what it's like to be laughed at and made fun of. I know what it's like to be insulted and have my self-esteem and confidence shot to pieces.

I know what it's like to feel like a giant puzzle, with one thousand fragmented pieces and somehow trying to figure out how they all connect to each other. My life is made up of fragments and slowly over the years, since my transformation, puzzle pieces have been coming together. Slowly I have snapped pieces together and a picture of who I am is forming. It will take some time to make a complete picture but what I've put together so far is rather nice.

I said it before and I'll say it here again that it's not easy. It is a constant fight to stay where I am. I think society places too much emphasis on being happy. It's an emotion just like sadness, anger, or joy. No one can be happy all the time. We can learn to be content with our lives but as I walk around town I see a lot of people that look like they're happy but their eyes say something else. You can see sorrow. We all present a certain view of ourselves to the world but when we do that how much of our true selves do we hide away and neglect? How much of ourselves do we sacrifice for others? How much do the people we surround ourselves with define who we are?

I think that was one of many issues for me during my depression and into my suicide attempts. I was letting other people define me instead of me defining myself. I didn't really know where to begin in defining myself. By letting others define me, well, it got me into trouble. People still try and define me or expect me to be a certain way and when I'm not I don't know what to say. I rode the elevator with a co-worker one day who asked me how I was and I said I was okay, They didn't really believe me because I didn't seem like my usual upbeat self. It's almost an expectation that I have to be a certain way all the time, but I can't. I can't be happy all the time, there are other emotions that I have and with my current medical condition I just say I'm okay for the hell of it. Most of my co-workers just accept that answer and go about their business but those closest to me know when I'm just saying okay to say it and that I'm really not okay at all.

My medical condition does take its toll on me. The side effects alone are a pain in my ass but while I deal with an internal organ that doesn't want to work like it's supposed to, I do what I can to remain sitting on this fence and look at the beautiful lush green meadow before me and not the dead swamp and forest behind me. My medical condition bums me out and at times it has heightened my need to cry and be held by someone. I mange my condition the best that I can but there are times where I'm so frustrated by it that I just want to crawl into my bed and just stay there.

Medical problem aside, I do my best to be like everyone else in the world, somewhat normal. I may not be happy all the time but I'm alive and that's better than being dead. Then again, I have no problem being dead and maybe that's because I've seen a glimpse of what could be. I am content with being alive because if I had succeeded in killing myself I would have missed out on meeting Michael and Keith, I would have missed out on meeting a lot of people who have come and gone from life.

I really don't know if my ramblings have served a purpose to anyone reading this except to read how messed up I was. I just hope that by shining a light on this subject that others won't ever feel so alone, and if they are alone, I hope they know that being alone is not an entirely a bad thing.

I think many of us make the mistake of ignoring how we feel because we think it's the wrong way to feel. For instance, when I started liking my friend's boyfriend I somehow convinced myself that those feelings were wrong. Amazingly, when I was depressed and drinking more than I should have been, I identified with Steve Clark and my feelings were suddenly validated by him. The biggest emotional denial we all experience is when someone dies. Men are expected not to cry and women are expected to fall apart. If you alter from the norm then something is wrong with you. This is exactly what my mom's family must have thought when I smiled instead of cried at my grandfather's funeral. What they didn't understand was that I already knew what was waiting for him and where he was. I knew he was in a good place.

I come from a family who is void of emotions. When I grew up I didn't get hugged by my parents, told "I love you" or offered words of encouragement. I had to depend on myself to become who I am now. I had to look to my environment to find myself. Make no mistake, I'm still trying to figure out who I am because I'm sure there are parts of myself I have yet to discover.

I took a big risk by exposing myself in this way and sharing my journey through darkness with you. I don't mind talking about what I went through but at times I do get weepy. I only hope that there is something here in these pages that might shed some light on your own life or at least make you understand something new about yourself. I didn't set out to cure depression and suicide or to tell someone not to do it. What I wanted most of all was to share with you, the reader, something that took me a while to find: hope.

I didn't know how to have it for myself. I had to be shown what hope was from a man who drowned his pain in a bottle. I had to be shown what hope was from a band that endured exceptionally tough times. It may sound silly, but hope, faith and belief that life can be better are viable concepts. Once you start to believe that your life is not worthless, that you are not alone, that you do have something to offer, something wonderful happens to you. You come alive.

EPILOGUE

Several months have passed since the initial writing of my story. A few revelations have surfaced as I continue to learn from my past. While I admit that a fair share was said about music in my story with a huge nod to Def Leppard, there were other bands that influenced me along the way. The majority of my healing was due to Def Leppard, but there was also another type of healing happening. While I'm sure music fans will cringe at me for even mentioning Def Leppard in the same sentence as Metallica, please understand that music is a universal language. It is the one language. It is the language that unites all of us, whether we admit it or not.

When I initially wrote this book, Def Leppard's music was playing in the background. It only made sense that the music that helped me get to a better place would be guiding me on this project. It wasn't until my book was off to the Editor that an afternoon spent watching Metallica's "Some Kind of Monster" documentary unlocked something in me. Something from my high school days that I had forgotten. In my senior year, the quote I picked to have under my name in the yearbook was from a Metallica song. If you are not familiar with the song "One" I highly suggest you look the lyrics up or better yet, find a copy of Metallica's "...And Justice for All" album. The first verse of that song is what I quoted in my yearbook. The entire song spoke to me because indeed I felt as if I was the only one, alone and trapped in a darkness that I didn't know how to escape. If there was ever a song that could sum up my seven years of depression and suicide, it's THAT song. There is no other song by any other artist that can capture or comment on the sad state of affairs that was my life back then.

After watching the movie and remembering the quote in my yearbook, other things about Metallica came to mind. The song, for starters, and then by accident I found a picture of drummer Lars Ulrich buried in a drawer with my Def Leppard paraphernalia. I sat there for a moment looking at the dated photo of him. It was a decent photo that I had obviously ripped out of some rock magazine given the uneven left edge. Not sure if it was another

Ross Halfin or Neil Zlozower masterpiece captured in black and white but nonetheless, the photo stirred something in me.

The aggressive, dark nature of Metallica's music spoke to a part of me as a teenager. Their music didn't fuel my desire to die. They were simply representing the **Saboteur's** dark nature. Their music reached my inner darkness; my inner pain. I have come to understand that while Metallica played to the darker, destructive aspects of myself, listening to the songs I identified with so strongly as a young adult does not evoke the same feelings now. Strangely enough, when I listen to these old songs, there is not a feeling of depression or darkness but of overall contentment.

Contentment in a Metallica song? I know. Sounds strange to say, but it's quite true. The troubled kid who hurt so much was disguised as a Metallica song. The **Saboteur** thrived on Metallica while *Inner Me* thrived on Def Leppard. Now, many years removed, all the parts of who I am thrive on Def Leppard and Metallica. Equally. They equally have my attention and perhaps this explains the contentment I feel when listening to Metallica songs. The battle that raged inside me for years has finally come to rest. The **Saboteur,** *Inner Me* and I have come to a compromise. We have called a truce.

Much like a band, all parts work in unison to create lyrics, harmony and melodies. All of these parts come together to make a song that reflects who we are. This is the song of ourselves. This is the song we sing to the universe. This is the song we share with others, who in turn share theirs with us.

My journey through the musical landscape of my youth is incomplete. Once I rediscovered Metallica, I rediscovered my love for Megadeth, too. I rediscovered my heavy metal/thrash side. At one time this music reflected a tormented soul but now the music just makes me want to rise up and scream with joy. I am listening to the music of my youth with new ears. There is a Megadeth song called "In My Darkest Hour" which I recently listened to again for the first time in twenty years. I cried. That song said everything I felt when I was younger but now I find a sense of comfort in it. In all honesty, I stopped listening to this kind of music for a long time and now that I have come back to it, I find that I really missed it. The music of Megadeth has made me feel welcomed back to a family I had almost forgotten. How I could have forgotten Dave Mustaine's intricate guitar work, snarling yet comforting voice—and inspiring, if not thought provoking lyrics is beyond me. He stirs something in me much in the same way Steve Clark does. He has made me realize that when we are in our darkest hours there is always a light burning deep inside us—even when we think it's gone.

I know that I wouldn't have survived my journey without music and I now only realize, as I sit back and reflect, that music has always spoken to me on a much deeper level. There is always a message for us if we are all willing to open our ears.

Epilogue

I have quite a way to go on my journey, but I am starting to see the pattern take hold. One band leads to another, which then leads me to another, leading me back to painful times only to heal me as I walk forward. Each band is like a breadcrumb that was dropped in the dark forest. These crumbs are guiding me to a beautiful meadow, with a beautiful little Irish cottage looking over the sea. Music has brought me home.

The story you have read is my song to all of you. I hope you find your own song and share it with the world. Someone out there is waiting, wanting and needing to hear it.

The journey continues. . .

APPENDIX

Chapter One: *I Never Liked The Rain Until I Walked Through It With You*
Song: Like the Rain **Album:** Greatest Hits **Artist:** Clint Black
Songwriter(s): Black/Hayden. ©1996 (BMI)

Chapter Two: *Light My Fire*
Song: Light My Fire **Album:** The Doors **Artist:** The Doors
Songwriter(s): Densmore/Krieger/Manzarek/Morrison ©1967 (ASCAP)

Chapter Three: *Ain't Too Funny When You'd Rather Die*
Song: Calling Card **Album:** Calling Card **Artist:** Rory Gallagher **Songwriter(s)**:Gallagher ©1976 (PRS/BMI)

Chapter Four: *Straight Jacket Memories, Sedative Highs*
Song: Eyes of a Stranger **Album:** Operation: Mindcrime **Artist:** Queensryche **Songwriter(s)**: DeGarmo/Tate ©1988 (BMI)

Chapter Five: *Bringin' On The Heartbreak*
Song: Bringin' On The Heartbreak **Album:** High 'N' Dry **Artist:** Def Leppard **Songwriter(s)**: Clark/Elliott/Willis ©1981 (ASCAP)

Chapter Six: *Don't Cry*
Song: Don't Cry **Album:** Seal **Artist:** Seal
Songwriter(s): Samuel ©1991 (BMI)

Chapter Seven: *It's Such A Magical Mysteria*
Song: Hysteria **Album:** Hysteria **Artist:** Def Leppard
Songwriter(s): Clark/Collen/Elliott/Lange/Savage ©1987 (ASCAP)

Chapter Eight: *Rock of Ages*
Song: Rock of Ages **Album:** Pyromania **Artist:** Def Leppard
Songwriter(s): Clark/Elliott/Lange ©1983 (ASCAP)

Chapter Nine: *Anybody Listening*
Song: Anybody Listening **Album:** Empire **Artist:** Queesryche
Songwriter(s): DeGarmo/Tate ©1990 (BMI)

Chapter Ten: *Don't Give Up On Me, I'm About To Come Alive*
Song: I'm About To Come Alive **Album:** My Private Nation **Artist:** Train
Songwriter(s): Bennett/Colin/Hotchkiss/Monahan/Stafford/Underwood
©2003 (ASCAP)

Chapter Eleven: *I Want To Know What Love Is*
Song: I Want To Know What Love Is **Album:** Agent Provocateur **Artist:**
Foreigner
Songwriter(s): Jones ©1984 (ASCAP)

Chapter Twelve: *From The Inside*
Song: From The Inside **Album:** Retro Active **Artist:** Def Leppard
Songwriter(s): Elliott ©1993 (ASCAP)

Chapter Thirteen: *To Be Alive*
Song: To Be Alive **Album:** Through Time **Artist:** Clock
Songwriter(s): Campbell/Smith ©1999 (BMI)

Chapter Fourteen: *Miss You In A Heartbeat*
Song: Miss You In A Heartbeat **Album:** Retro Active **Artist:** Def Leppard **Songwriter(s):** Collen ©1993 (ASCAP)

Chapter Fifteen: *There's Still Time To Change The Road You're On*
Song: Stairway to Heaven **Album:** Led Zeppelin IV **Artist:** Led Zeppelin
Songwriter(s): Page/Plant ©1971 (ASCAP)

Chapter Sixteen: *It's Just An Angel Whose Wings Hide The Sun*
Song: All I Want Is Everything **Album:** Slang **Artist:** Def Leppard
Songwriter(s): Elliott ©1996

Chapter Seventeen: *I Walk Alone In The Darkness Of The City*
Song: Stranger In This Town **Album:** Stranger In This Town **Artist:**
Richie Sambora **Songwriter(s):** Bryan/Sambora ©1991 (ASCAP)

Chapter Eighteen: *Livin' Is The Best Revenge You Can Play*
Song: Blood Runs Cold **Album:** Slang **Artist:** Def Leppard
Songwriter(s): Collen/Elliott ©1996

Chapter Nineteen: *Long, Long Way To Go*
Song: Long, Long Way To Go **Album:** X **Artist:** Def Leppard
Songwriter(s): Hall/Robson ©2002 (ASCAP)

www.ingramcontent.com/pod-product-compliance
Lightning Source LLC
Chambersburg PA
CBHW022306060426
42446CB00007BA/634